CHRISTIAN BASICS

Christian Basics

A PRIMER FOR PILGRIMS

Dorothy and Gabriel Fackre

WILLIAM B. EERDMANS PUBLISHING COMPANY
GRAND RAPIDS, MICHIGAN

Copyright © 1991 by Wm. B. Eerdmans Publishing Co.
255 Jefferson Ave. S.E., Grand Rapids, Mich. 49503

Printed in the United States of America

Library of Congress Cataloging-in-Publication Data

Fackre, Dorothy, 1924 –
    Christian basics: a primer for pilgrims / Dorothy and Gabriel Fackre.
      p.   cm.
    Includes index.
    ISBN 0-8028-0541-8
    1. Theology, Doctrinal — Popular works.   I. Fackre, Gabriel J.
II. Title.
BT77.F28   1991
230 — dc20
                                        90-27066
                                          CIP

Scripture quotations are from the New Revised Standard Version, copyright
© 1989 by the Division of Christian Education of the National Council of
the Churches of Christ in the United States of America. Used by permission.

For Ben, Gilowen, Acacia
and cousins to come

Contents

Foreword   viii

Prologue: God   1

1. Creation   5

2. The Fall   18

3. Covenant   27

4. Jesus Christ   38

5. The Church   64

6. Salvation   90

7. Consummation   125

Epilogue: God   141

Afterword   155

Glossary / Index   163

Foreword

What's life all about? Is it worth trying to do right? What *is* right? Is there any hope? Can we believe in *anything?* Yes, we can!

When people ask the hard questions, it's time to go "back to the basics." Especially so when many are ready to believe almost anything — the bizarre stories in the supermarket tabloid, the latest theories of the talk-show host, the spiritualist saga of the movie star.

The authors of this book believe that Christian faith makes a lot more sense of life than the fads and frenzies of the hour. And we are talking about "the faith" as it is believed in garden-variety Christianity. We have taken what we know about it and put it down here for people who want a refresher course in Christian basics.

The basics are found in the Book. To the extent that folk have lost touch with this biblical Charter, it's a matter of going *back* to the basics. But, in a sense, the basics are really not behind but in front. "Ever-*new* light and truth shall break from God's holy Word." So said Pastor Robinson when he sent the Pilgrims on their way across the waters. The old,

old Story takes on fresh meaning with each new circumstance. And for those who never learned about the faith, the direction definitely lies ahead. *Forward* to the basics!

This "primer for pilgrims" is organized as a "story" because God's dealings with humankind are sheer drama. They run from the beginning of the world to its end — "creation" to "consummation." We taught our children that way in a catechism we wrote for them.[1] And Gabe has taken up the theme for pastors and students in his *Christian Story* series.[2] As the song goes, "We've a story to tell to the nations!"

Rather than telling personal stories drawn from our experience, we decided instead to concentrate on the Big Story.[3] The times cry out for it. That's the message that comes from the shopping-mall bookstore shelves marked "religion and the occult," which are filled with the latest oracles on life, death, and destiny. This book is an alternative vision of the way the world works — the ABCs of basic Christianity, strong and straight doses of its doctrine.

We try to tell the Big Story as it is believed in most churches. While it is always found in a variety of versions, there is a common thread of teaching. We trace it as best we can. But the reader knows that it comes through our filter too, and therefore corrections and adaptations have to be made.[4] But by writing it together, we've made an effort to

1. Gabriel and Dorothy Fackre and family, "A Catechism for Today's Storytellers," *Youth* 23 (July 1972): 23-42.
2. See *The Christian Story: A Narrative Interpretation of Basic Christian Doctrine*, rev. ed. (Grand Rapids: Wm. B. Eerdmans, 1984); and *The Christian Story*, vol. 2: *Authority: Scripture in the Church for the World* (Grand Rapids: Wm. B. Eerdmans, 1987).
3. We are going to tell those stories in a companion volume to *Christian Basics*.
4. For a glimpse of the background and perspective of the co-authors,

widen the angle of vision. The contents have been tested with many laity and clergy. Especially helpful was a 1989 study group at the Craigville Conference Center in Massachusetts that pushed us hard to be down-to-earth.

The language that Christians use to tell their Story has its own mysterious dialect. The Glossary-Index at the back of the book defines some Christian code words. And to go deeper into any topic, the reader may want to do some background study in the companion volumes of *The Christian Story;* near the end of each chapter in this book there are references to corresponding sections in those volumes. This language is extremely important: mainline/oldline churches will not experience renewal until they have relearned their own language.

Over the centuries, the Bible's special language has been formed into "doctrines," the basic convictions of the church. That's another way of describing the contents of this book. Christian basics are Christian *doctrines.* "Theology" is the church's talk about them, especially as they are put into the setting of a given time and place. These teachings are "chapters" in the greatest story ever told. In addition to describing these doctrines, we indicate what they have meant for Christians in the daily life of action and spirituality (an emphasis that is particularly strong in the chapter on salvation).

When we were serving a parish in Pittsburgh in the 1950s, we wrote a book together, *Under the Steeple,* dedicated to our parents. *Christian Basics* is dedicated to our grandchildren. In the first book we were very conscious of our debt to forebears. Now the future looms large. We think of the generation to come. May there be no nuclear winter for them.

---

see the autobiographical section of the second volume of *The Christian Story,* pp. 3-41.

And no winter of faith either. May they know the Shalom that God has promised! Tell them the Story.

What follows previews things to come.

How the Dawn Came

A Short Story

In the beginning, God had a dream. The world is bathed in the divine Light. Creation and Creator are at one. There is joy and peace in Eden.

Some have pictured it as a campfire scene. God is the roaring blaze. Humanity is a circle of dancers, arms linked, eyes watching each other, at home in the silent woods, celebrating the fire-Light.

But reality shatters the dream. The people love Night more than Light. So all in the circle spin around on their heels, drawn by the Powers of Darkness. The about-face breaks the bonds. Facing outward, the people can't find each other anymore. Nor can they see the Light. Nature takes on a fearsome look as the distorted shadows of the lonely dancers play on the forest round about. This is not what God wanted! The "wages of sin" are the death of the dream.

The dream, though, will not die. A spark from the blaze finds its way to each dancer. An inner light keeps alive God's Hope. In each there is a flickering "image of God." Will that glow turn the world around?

God's long-suffering Love will not let us go. More light comes — a rainbow sign! A promise that God will not give up on us. And more — a path shown to a promised land . . . and a people called! The breath of God blows on a spark and brings into being a "pillar of fire" to lead Israel away from Night toward the true Light. To this people comes the law of a new land, commandments of turning to God and neighbor. In the people's midst rises a company of visionaries — prophets, seers of Light. They point to freedom and peace — Shalom — a world where the circle is reknit, where swords are beaten into plowshares, where wolf and lamb lie down together!

But the people wander and go astray. Their prophets declare that the Day of the Lord will be Darkness, not Light.

Yet God keeps promises. Shalom *will* come to pass!

What will turn our willful world around? Sparks and pillars do not do it. We must be found *firsthand*.

The people who walk in darkness see a great Light. The dream becomes *flesh* and dwells among us, "full of grace and truth." Light shines in the face of Jesus Christ! We behold its glory. Shalom is born in Bethlehem . . . and lives in Galilee. The sick are healed. Justice is done. Sin is forgiven. Good News is preached. Hope is kindled. The Realm of God is *here* as well as near. Christ our liberator has come! Christ is our peace — the Light of the *world*.

When Light comes close to those in the grip of gloom, it sears the flesh. Shalom in our midst shames our shut-up ways. Love's coals burn the enemies of Light. The disarrayed dancers recoil. The powers of evil brace for battle. On a lonely hill, Night again descends; Christ is crucified; the Dream dies.

"On the first day of the week, at early dawn, they came to the tomb. . . ." Empty! Death can*not* bury the Dream! On the cross, the powers of death meet their match! Sin is forgiven! Easter heralds the defeat of Night. Christ is risen . . . a new *Day* breaks.

The Dawnburst makes its mark. Its rays warm the backs

of the wandering dancers. Some slowly turn . . . and sight the Sun. They see the Light!

With Light comes Life. They live by its power, in faith — trusting in the mercy of God, hoping for the Not Yet, pilgrims on a new path.

An about-face to the Horizon brings new vision. Dawn People discern the neighbor in need. They see *by the Light* as well as *see the Light.* And they cannot pass by the wretched of the earth.

Dawnlight brings pilgrims together. They see the brother and sister in Christ as well as the forgotten and forlorn. No solo travelers; they form a family. And to others they call, "Come join us to see this Light and follow this Way!"

Dawn is not Noonday. There are still shadows on the land. Sin persists and death is our common lot. The promise fills the sky, but the meridian when all the clouds are gone awaits a Yet to Be.

As we live in the half-light of an already–not yet, God's Story merges with our stories. We now become characters in the unfolding plot — seeing the Light, seeing our companions in it, seeing the victims on the Jericho road *by* it, and pointing others *to* it.

And so unfolds the marvelous Story we have to tell, the song we have to sing:

> The darkness shall turn to the dawning,
> And the dawning to noonday bright.
> And Christ's great kingdom shall come to earth,
> The kingdom of love and light!

THE STORY . . . LINE

Prologue: God

The Tale begins in eternity with the triune God — "Father, Son, and Holy Spirit." The three lines representing them form the symbol found in church architecture:

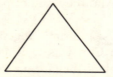

Chapter I: Creation

God calls the world into being — into being together as the triune God is. The Great Invitation: God (first line) reaches out to the world (second line):

Chapter II: The Fall

The world says "No!" to the invitation. Estrangement occurs.

Chapter III: Covenant

God seeks to reclaim us, stretching toward

    — all the world in the covenant with Noah, the rainbow sign:

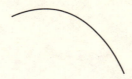

    — the chosen people, Israel, in the promise to Abraham and the exodus from Egypt:

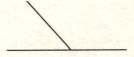

Chapter IV: Jesus Christ

God drives deep into the world as the Word becomes flesh and dwells among us — to live and die, and to rise again:

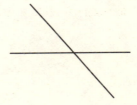

Chapters V . . . VI . . . VII: The Church, Salvation, Consummation

The power of God, the Holy Spirit, takes the victory won in Christ and draws the world toward the divine purpose:

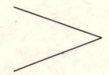

Epilogue: God

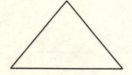

PROLOGUE

God

WHO IS GOD?

To get a story started, we need to know something about its cast of characters. In the Christian Story, that means learning something about its chief figure — God. Hence this Prologue.

The Book of our Story says, "In the beginning God . . ." (Gen. 1:1), and "In the beginning was the Word" (John 1:1). It also says there is a "secret purpose framed from the very beginning" (1 Cor. 2:7, NEB). God — with a Word, a Purpose. God . . . "had a dream"! For Christians that Dream came true, the Purpose was fulfilled, the Word was spoken in *Jesus*. So, with the Bible, as with any book or play that lists its characters in the beginning, we have to anticipate what is to come.

We all have purposes, plans, and hopes. Like Martin Luther King, Jr., we say, "I have a dream!" But human hopes are often dashed. King was cruelly shot down. Expectations meet harsh reality. Our dreams may falter and our visions fail, but it's different with Deity. God has the *power* to fulfill the divine purpose. God is a Purposer with a Purpose and the *Power* to fulfill it. Even when the Dream is destroyed, it comes right back!

1

THE TRIUNE GOD

Purposer . . . Purpose . . . Power. Notice how these three words match up with some ancient words in the Story: Purposer = "Father," Purpose = "Son," Power = "Spirit." God is "Father, Son, and Spirit."[1]

We have just met a part of the basic Christian belief in God: the *Trinity*. God's "threeness" is tied up with the Christian experience of God as (1) the Creator and Purposer of the world (2) whose Purpose came among us as Jesus Christ, and (3) who sent the Power, the Holy Spirit, to see the Purpose through. These are three great acts in the biblical drama, recorded, for example, in the three paragraphs of the Apostles' and Nicene creeds. But for Christians, God is not just first one, then the other, and then the other — but all three at the same time.

When we use terms like "Word," "Purpose," and "Power," they sound impersonal. When the Bible uses them, they're not. They have a life of their own. The eternal Word of God, the eternal Purpose of God, *lives* and *acts*. The Holy

---

1. Using language that does not exclude women or other groups is an important Christian commitment. We have tried to be sensitive to that throughout this book. Almost all biblical citations are from the New Revised Standard Version of the Bible (1989), which reflects this concern. While using inclusive language for humankind is becoming a widespread practice, language for God presents a fresh set of critical issues. Some would conjoin "Goddess" with "God," or eliminate the word "God" on the grounds of its masculine gender origins. We reject that option. "God" is the proper name for deity in the Christian faith, with gender associations long gone. (See Gabriel Fackre, "God, Understandings of," in *The Encyclopedia of Religious Education*, ed. Kendig and Iris Cully [San Francisco: Harper & Row, 1990], pp. 271-73.) We have used "God," the name of the One with whom we have to do, with inclusive intent in the place of pronouns. And we have retained the traditional Trinitarian language for the divine name with its biblical warrant and ecumenical usage.

Spirit does too. The Spirit and the Son are as *personal* as the Father. God is "triune" — one God in *three* "Persons"! And the Three are so *together* that God is not a "They" but a "Thou." They live *in* each other so that the Three are really One. Or, in the simple words of the Bible, "God *is* love" (1 John 4:8, our italics).

But how could this one God be at the same time Three? A pious believer once said, "You either lose your mind trying to figure it out, or lose your soul denying it!"

We shall return to this question in the Epilogue, after the Story is told. *Who* God is becomes clearer when we hear *what* God does, when the whole Tale is told. For now, we need to know that the great drama about to unfold grows out of the will and way of the triune God. God *does* what God *is:* Life Together. That means the very being of God has something to do with the Purpose for which the world is made. We are brought into being to pursue *this* Vision, made to fulfill *this* Dream of life together with God and one another. How that plan develops, its ups and downs, is the story to come.[2]

WHERE DO WE GO TO FIND OUT?

In this Prologue we make mention of *where* we find the Story as well as *who* its Author and chief Actor are. The Story is found in the Book. The *Bible* is the source of our knowledge of *who God is, what God does, who we are,* and *where we are headed.*

For 1900 years the church has struggled with the con-

2. Cf. *The Christian Story,* rev. ed. (Grand Rapids: Wm. B. Eerdmans, 1984), pp. 56-67.

3

tents of this Book. The divisions within the church have a lot to do with disagreements about what the Book means. Therefore, what the church has said about the faith is part of the "where" of the matter. So too is the world of experience that everyone in the church brings to the reading of the Bible. We have placed this discussion of Bible/church/world in the Afterword of this book. The reader may want to refer to it from time to time. Questions about the *interpretation of the Bible*, the *authority of the church*, and the *place of human experience in our faith* crop up all along the line.

Now it's time for the adventure.

QUESTIONS TO CONSIDER

1. Has the Trinity been a vital part of Christian belief for you? Why or why not?

2. What are some symbols for the Trinity that appear in stained-glass windows and church furnishings?

3. Are there hints in human experience of the unity of three-in-one? The church over the centuries has been hesitant about pushing these hints too hard as analogies for the Trinity. Why do you think this has been the case? (Think about a few of them: H_2O as water, ice, and vapor; a person playing different roles; three individuals who share the same nature.)

4. What do the creeds, confessions, catechisms, and/or statements of faith in your tradition say about the Trinity?

5. Why has the Trinity been so important in Christian faith over the centuries? Come back to this question when you've finished reading this Story.

I

Creation

Why the world? Why is there something and not nothing? Why, why, why? Philosophers say such a question is the beginning of wisdom.

How did it all happen? *When* did the world begin? *Where* was the first sign of life? With telescopes and microscopes, scientists spend their days pondering these questions, just as philosophers pose theirs.

The Christian Story begins differently. It is interested in another kind of question: *Who* brought the world to be? *What* does it all mean? The Book puts its answer very simply:

> In the beginning when God created the heavens and the earth. . . . God saw everything that he had made, and indeed, it was very good. (Gen. 1:1, 31)

It all began with God. That's who made it — the One we talked about in the Prologue. And if God made it, then the world must be *good*. Stones and stars, animals and humans, atoms and genes, powers and processes — all bear the stamp of God's approval. And that means it's all here for a purpose.

We get a glimpse of that plan in Genesis, the first book of the Bible. The Creator makes a garden and puts people in it. They are asked to tend the garden, and are called to live in loyalty to God and in love one to another. "Paradise" exists for life together — just like the Life Together in God! The garden is a picture the Bible gives us of God's intention for us.

What happened to this Dream is something else again. It didn't turn out very well. We'll get to that in the next chapter. For now, we'll concentrate on God's will for the world, a wonderful hope portrayed vividly in the early scenes of the Bible. Of course the Will and the Hope are painted in picture language and according to the science of that day and age. We must tune in to the writer's wish to tell us about the *Who* and the *What* instead of making the Bible answer the scientists' and philosophers' questions of How, Why, When, and Where. That's what it means to hear "the Word" — the Bible is speaking to us. Let's listen for it now.

NATURE

The first twenty-five verses of the Bible are about day and night, water and land, birds and beasts. God liked the results of creation:

> God saw that it was good. (Gen. 1:25)

A second version of the world's beginnings in chapter 2 makes the same point. Here we learn of the flowing rivers and flowering trees that were "pleasant to the sight and good for food" (Gen. 2:9).

This enthusiasm for the good earth at the beginning of the Bible is matched by a celebration of its fulfillment at the very end of the Bible:

> Then I saw a new heaven and a new earth . . . the river of the water of life, bright as crystal . . . the tree of life with its twelve kinds of fruit . . . no more night . . . for the Lord God will be their light. (Rev. 21:1; 22:1, 2, 5)

These wonders of *nature* are made for a life of peace with each other and with God. One of the Bible's prophets speaks of it as the wolf living with the lamb, the leopard and the kid lying down together (Isa. 11:6). And nature is even designed to be in harmony with humans: the child befriends the snake (Isa. 11:8), and the leaves of the tree of life "are for the healing of the nations" (Rev. 22:2).

All well and good, "in the beginning" and at the end. How about now? Right now, nature is full of *pain*, "red in tooth and claw" (as Tennyson said), for "the whole creation has been groaning" (Rom. 8:22).

Yet the good God watches over the good earth. The care is right there for those with the eyes to see:

> The heavens are telling the glory of God; and the firmament proclaims his handiwork. (Ps. 19:1)

And Jesus too tells us to

> Consider the lilies of the field, how they grow; they neither toil nor spin; yet I tell you, even Solomon in all his glory was not clothed like one of these. (Matt. 6:28-29)

All well and good, again. But we must remember that "good" is not *God*. Sometimes nature puts us under its spell.

7

The blue vault above, the radiance of a spring morning, the eagles' flight, the sandpipers' trail . . . glorious! The thunder's rumble, the crashing wave, the limitless canopy of stars . . . awe-inspiring! So much so that ancients *worshipped* sun, sea, and stars. Some people today do too. Not so in the Christian Story. The good earth, yes. Commune with it, delight in its beauties, investigate its designs. But worship is for the *Creator*, not the creation. When soil or blood or sea or sun get to the worship stage, we are in trouble. The Holocaust of Hitler's blood-and-soil natur*ism* shows us what can happen.

Ecology, Science, and Mystery

Christians have a poor record of practicing what they preach about the good earth. If we had done better, the eagles and flowers, the soil and the trees would not be in the trouble they are today. The Story should put its tellers in the front ranks of those eager to make the deserts bloom. Some *are* on the ecological frontline, but the rest of us have a long way to go.

Creation teaching *has* made a difference in other places. Science, for one, is in the Story's debt, although little notice is taken of that debt in today's textbooks. The Story taught us that because the earth is good, its patterns are worth examining. While nature shouldn't be worshipped, it should be investigated. And if the Creator is "together," creation must be orderly, too. Where that has been proclaimed, science has taken rise. The earth is to be honored by the study of its ways. Except, of course, when we don't practice what we preach. Then we persecute the Galileos.

When talking about science and the Bible, we should

remind ourselves of the distinction between the Who and What concerns of the believer and the How, Why, When, and Where interests of the scientist. While Genesis borrows the science of its day (the world made in six days about the year 4004 B.C., according to Bishop Usher's adding up the ages of people in the Old Testament genealogies), it does so in order to make its main points about Who created the world and What it is made up of — nature, human nature, supernature. Failure to distinguish between these two kinds of issues has caused people to miss the doctrine and concentrate instead on its wrappings. (How to read the Bible is discussed in more detail in the Afterword.)

God made the world to be a good partner. Nature, like everything else, is invited to praise God. Here's a vision of how it ought to be:

> I heard every creature in heaven and on earth and under the earth and in the sea, and all that is in them, singing, "To the one seated on the throne and to the Lamb be blessing and honor and glory and might forever and ever!" (Rev. 5:13)

Nature praising God! Odd. Can it "decide" such things? We don't think about nature that way. It just follows the rules, "natural laws." But the more the scientist probes into the depths of things, the more difficult it is to talk about rules. And philosophers have begun to speculate about the "withinness" of things. At its most basic levels, nature seems to have a spontaneity. Whatever the electron microscopes discover, or however the modern philosopher speculates, the Christian Story has all along told us that every created thing can cry "Blessing and honor and glory and might" to God! Maybe not just like we can — remember the Bible's poetic license. But somehow! That way of looking at nature is one more reason to walk with wonder through the world.

HUMAN NATURE: THE IMAGE OF GOD

In the world's birth throes, a new character appears on the scene. A very special one, for

> God said, "Let us make humankind in our image." (Gen. 1:26)

The "image of God" is given to humans. What is it? Theologians, and philosophers too, have long puzzled over that. It's what makes human beings different. Is it something in us called "reason"? Is it "spirit"? Is it being a "tool-making animal"? Are we the only creatures that can laugh? Theories abound.

Relationship

As we have said, in the Christian Story, God is *Life Together.* To be the "image" of the One-in-Three must have something to do with that. To be made in God's image is to be made for *that same life together.* Human beings as those created in God's image are made in and for *relationship* — with God the giver of the image, and with one another as partners in it. The uniqueness of our human race rests finally on having this relationship: God bonding with us in the drama that is unfolding. Being human is being the apple of God's eye. Every self is special because of that unique call and claim. Human dignity has nothing to do with any quality or characteristic we have which if absent would make us lose that dignity (race, class, sex, age, physical / mental / emotional condition, intelligence, virtue, etc.). The sanctity of human life is unconditional, ours by sheer "grace."

Relationship is a gift, and it is an expectation. God "setteth the solitary in families," says the old King James Bible (Ps. 68:6). We are made to be "family." Indeed, that's the way Genesis puts it:

> So God created humankind in his image, in the image of God he created them; male and female he created them. (Gen. 1:27)

The Bible uses family imagery to talk about sacred things. It's the clearest picture we have of personal closeness in God and among ourselves. Scripture goes so far as to say that in marriage two people become "one flesh" (Gen. 2:24)! So God's Life Together becomes a pattern for our own life together on this earth, with the unity of the conjugal bond being a symbol of that.

Capacity

For humans, the unity of life with life depends on *choosing it*. It isn't just "doing what comes naturally." As in God, so in us: life together is born of *love*. "Imaging God" is living the loving life together. When we answer the call to mirror the very Being of God, a freely chosen life together, we are carrying out the expectation of our image. And that in-dwelling one of another ripples out from the most intimate relationship of a man and a woman to family, community, society, nation, the whole world. It has to do not only with other people but with nature too — harmony with other created beings. And, finally and fundamentally, it has to do with life together with *God*.

As in God, so in us. Total communion with the Other is born of a *will* to love. That's why "freedom," "reason," "choice," and "spirit" have been associated with the image of God in us. We do have this unique *capacity* as part of the image in which we are made. To be together in love as God is, we must be free to love — free to be together. Humans are special in this way too. Spontaneity (which can be found even in the depths of nature) comes to full flower as this capacity for freedom, for thinking and deciding, in humans. So the Story takes place on this terrain, beginning with God's Great Invitation to respond in love to God's love. The highest expression of this flowered freedom is what we call "spirit" — the freedom to love God and the world.

But we get things upside down if we focus only on the capacity and forget the relationship. The capacity is there because of the primal bonding of God to this thread of fragile human life in the world. And the capacity is there for a purpose. We are stewards of this freedom given by grace in order that we may take responsibility for *togethering* — with God and with the world.

Soul

What is it? Again, the answers have come thick and fast. Often "soul" is thought of as something in us, such as reason or spirit. Sometimes it is spoken of as the part of us that survives after our body dies. If we think of the image in which we are made primarily as God's relationship to us, then "soul" takes on a meaning that does not exclude the truth in popular understandings but stays closer to biblical usage.

The writer of 3 John says to its receiver, Gaius,

Beloved, I pray that all may go well with you and that you may be in good health, just as it is well with your soul. (v. 2)

"Soul" refers to Gaius-before-God. His soul is his self in its *singular* relationship to its Creator. And that includes its condition, the result of the way Gaius has employed the capacity of freedom given to him. A soul that is well is one with God. What constitutes that wellness — the grace that heals through faith — we shall soon examine. For now, it's important to understand that "soul" is the unique self you are, a one-and-only being-before-God, called to and capacitated for life together.

HUMAN NATURE: CREATURELINESS

We are made in the image of God *but* with a big difference. God is Creator; we are creatures. Our image is not free-floating but bound up with something else. We are human *nature*. We do not soar in our freedom like God but are tied to the earth — mortal and visible, not "immortal and invisible." The Psalms comment on our mortal state:

The days of our life are seventy years, or perhaps eighty, if we are strong. (Ps. 90:10)

Like flowers of the field we flourish, but then we wither and die. And the place knows us no more. This is the second part of Christian teaching about human nature: our *creatureliness*.

Humans are made in God's image, yes, but we are not eternal like God. And a reminder of that is our ever-so-fragile condition. The creature on whom the eye of God rests still needs food, clothing, and shelter, and is tied to humble and

13

earthy functions like urinating and defecating. What a combination of "grandeur and misery"! Knowing we are made for life with God yet being aware of our mortality unsettles us, makes us anxious. But it also ennobles us, for the special mix of "the image" and creatureliness means that life is more than eating and drinking, sex is more than biology, and our threescore years and ten are not the end.

To recognize and honor our creatureliness and its goodness in the plan of God is to acknowledge that people need food, clothing, and shelter, and that anything that deprives them of it — hunger, poverty, pollution, homelessness, injustice, tyranny, war — is against the will of God. And because the body and the spirit are so tightly interconnected in the Bible's teaching, the spirit of the image suffers when the body is hurt. (The body reflects the spirit's ups and downs, too.) So Christians care about all the forces of society that impact bodies and spirits, and watch and work for just and righteous conditions.

SUPERNATURE

The "supernatural"! From time to time, talk of it sweeps through society. Bizarre stories fascinate the readers of the checkout-counter press. Famous people reveal their belief in enchanted happenings. Films depict the horrifying unknown. New cults arise, with ghastly rituals. Scientists weigh the evidence of inexplicable events.

Sometimes the Bible is cited to back up claims about the supernatural. Aren't its pages full of devils and angels? And the Bible teaches too that there are ways of wrestling with angels and exorcizing demons.

Yes, the story of Creation is incomplete without a third cast of characters — the inhabitants of the realm of "supernature." Here dwell realities that are still part of the created order but are *more than* human.

Even seeing-is-believing skeptics never doubt some of this superhuman world. Forces are at work — social, economic, and political — that take on a life of their own. Necessary for human existence itself, they include such "orders of creation" as the family, the state, the economic order, and the institutions within and beyond them. Then there are the more intimate realities too, described by psychologists and portrayed by poets, that work in us and take possession of us. Scripture has its own language for these realities — "powers and principalities," "thrones and authorities" (Rom. 8:38; Col. 1:16, RSV).

Aren't these things merely impersonal factors in our life? So a secular world thinks. But the Story tells us of a world alive, from bottom to top. The powers are created by God and accountable to God. And believers in all ages have wrestled with their temptations and rejoiced in their support. That is why the powers are described in personal terms. Scripture speaks of "angels" — messengers of God (Ps. 91:11; Matt. 28:5; Heb. 13:2). They appear, speak, smite, encamp, ask and answer, wrestle, warn, descend, ascend. No full account of the Story can leave them out. Nor can the heavenly *realm* of supernature in which they live . . . and the departed dwell . . . be omitted. To the latter we shall return in chapters to come.

Christians argue among themselves about how literal we should be in our personal description of the powers. Can we throw an inkwell at one, as Luther did? Or do we go along with modernity and treat the powers as myth? Or is

15

there something in between? Whatever we think about that, there is no question that powers of supernature as well as the persons of human nature are players in the biblical drama. Indeed, they are related to Christ himself:

> For in him all things in heaven and on earth were created, things visible and invisible, whether thrones or dominions or rulers or powers — all things have been created through him and for him. (Col. 1:16)

So the More-than-human joins the human and natural in being called into being by the triune God to live in partnership with one another and their Creator.[1]

$$*\qquad\qquad *\qquad\qquad *$$

Creation is made by God, for God. Its characters at all levels of life — nature, human nature, and supernature — assemble themselves on the path toward the future. (In technical terms, we have just looked at the doctrines of "cosmology," "anthropology," and "angelology.") Creation stands poised for pilgrimage. How will the journey fare?

QUESTIONS TO CONSIDER

1. What effect does believing the Christian doctrine of creation have on one's attitude toward nature?

1. Cf. *The Christian Story*, rev. ed. (Grand Rapids: Wm. B. Eerdmans, 1984), pp. 68-76.

2. Some believe that "creationism" is a necessary part of Christian belief. What do you think?

3. Some believe that making a distinction between humanity and nature helps to destroy the environment and violate animal rights. What do you think?

4. What does it mean to say humans are made in "the image of God"? What are the ethical implications of this statement?

5. What does it mean to say humans are "creatures"? What are the ethical implications of this statement?

6. Do you see any connection between the rise of science and the biblical understanding of creation?

7. What is your view of angels, principalities, and powers?

8. Does the Christian faith have a response to occult teaching about the supernatural? Continue to think about this question as you study the Story.

II

The Fall

The call is given, the invitation extended. The world is beckoned to be together with its Creator. We visualized it in our simple line diagram this way:

——————— ———————

And the response? A flat "No!" to God's "Yes!" The world shakes its fist in the face of its Maker.

The story of this rejection is in Genesis, the book of beginnings. Christians read it in the light of the whole Bible, the New Testament included. It comes with vivid images, striking characters, and dramatic events: a forbidden tree, a seductive serpent, Adam and Eve tempted to overstep their bounds, face-saving moves and cover-ups, an angry Maker, an ousting from Paradise into a cold, cruel world (Gen. 3).

The church has never been able to forget the lesson of "the Fall." Thus its doctrine of "harmatology." Sometimes it has missed the point by debating the details: Was there really a talking snake? A special tree? God walking in a garden? (No, say the "modernists"; Yes, say the "fundamentalists"). Here we go again! The point is not the where and how of the matter but the *that* and *what*.

The big That is the heart of this chapter of the Story. The chance God gave the world to live a life together was — and is — turned down. *Strangely* turned down. Why, when we have everything to gain, does the world from the beginning of time say "No" to its Maker? There is no answer to this Why. It's the "mystery of iniquity." We can't explain it. But we *can* explore it. The Story gives us some clues.

That the world stumbled and fell rather than ran to embrace its Creator sets up the plot we are following. Here is the tension that cries out for resolution. The word for that tension is *Sin*.

When we think about the setting of the unfolding narrative, we see how silly a lot of talk about it is. Sin is a *chapter* in the Story, not a failure to live up to our favorite list of dos and don'ts. Sin is the awesome No to God. Let's consider what that means.

SIN AND EVIL

Idolatry

The whole world stumbles and falls, and human beings are at the center of this collapse. Nature and supernature are in

19

the picture too. But the focus is on humans — "Adam and Eve." Made in the very image of God, they are special. Their "Nay" looms large in the Story.

The Bible's account of sin in the first humans is a mirror held up to you and me. We were already there, so to speak, in our ancestors. What they did is exactly what we do—"original sin." Iniquity crops up all along the line — at the start of the Story, at its end, and right now. To ring a change on a popular spiritual, we *were* "there when they crucified my Lord."

What did/do we do? This big ego of ours is put off by God's dream. We want to go our own way, pursue our own purpose. Love God? Love the neighbor? Forget it!

To put ourselves center stage in the unfolding Drama is to displace the chief Character. We want to "play God"! That's exactly the way sin is described in Genesis. The serpent tempts Adam and Eve to "be like God" (Gen. 3:5). We want to be Number One; indeed, sin is "looking out for Number One." But that place is already occupied. To covet it is to put ourselves where God alone belongs. When we make ourselves the center of the universe, we have put the creature in the place of the Creator. What else is that but worshipping an idol instead of the true God? Sin, at bottom, is self-worship — *idolatry*. The ancients called it *hubris*, the pride that plays God.

Taking God's place has consequences for the rest of the world. As we elevate ourselves, we want others to bow the knee to us. What else when we play God? We make others our subjects. *Arrogance* is the child of idolatry.

Arrogance and the Will to Power

Arrogance is "lording it over" others, putting them down. This sin is the special temptation of the powerful. Lord Acton had it right: "Power tends to corrupt, and absolute power corrupts absolutely." While the arrogant really have only a smidgen of power, they mistake it for the Power of God and throw their small weight around. Here sin is the pride of the powerful.

The arrogance of power takes its toll on the powerless. But sooner or later it backfires on the usurper. As the Book puts it,

[God] has brought down the powerful from their thrones, and lifted up the lowly. (Luke 1:52)

Arrogance is also the special sin of the spirit. The very aspect of the self that is kindred to God — the freedom to be together, the "capacity" of the divine image in us — is susceptible to corruption. We are regularly tempted to think more highly than we ought to of ourselves. It's no accident that the "righteous" were the foes of Jesus! Spiritual power is the severest temptation. Righteousness becomes *self-righteousness* and exclaims, "God, I thank you that I am not like other people!" (Luke 18:11). Virtue becomes a smokescreen for self-elevation. Piety and morality are ever and again the occasion for a prideful power.

Apathy and Escape

Sin takes other forms. Idolatry works itself out in *apathy* as well as arrogance. Those *out of power* are susceptible to this kind of temptation. Here self-centeredness barricades itself into its throne room by refusal to risk. So we *escape* from freedom, refusing to decide . . . letting events take their course. We blame our circumstances just as the first human characters in the Story faulted the snake and each other. Yet apathy itself is a choice, the decision *not to act*.

The flight from decision can take an even more earthy direction — a headlong rush into *sensuality*. While the word can be used differently today, the old Christian writers meant by it the propensity to make the body the be-all and end-all of our life. Satisfying its desires becomes the purpose of living. Gluttony, lavish outfits, and fancy quarters — all are perversions of the legitimate needs for food, clothing, and shelter. Lust, promiscuity, and perversity — these are abuses of a God-blessed sexuality. Drugs and alcohol — these deaden the senses and allow us to live in a fantasy world. Sin in this form is the drowning of the human spirit in the ocean of our natural existence.

The sins of arrogance and apathy correspond to the twin aspects of the self: the image of God and creatureliness. Behind each is the narcissism of the "I" with its own home in the spirit. So the Christian faith is very sober about the state of sin, traceable as it is to the most precious gift given to the human race, the very reflection of deity.

And the Christian faith has no illusions about sin's pervasiveness. That's why it talks about "original sin." "Original" means that our lethal tendency has been there from the beginning, from the moment humans had the option to choose — to go the way of the "serpent" or the way of God. And since then, that inclination to play God has been ever with us. Our will has been "in bondage" to our self-seeking, has been unfree, in that sense, to do the good. The Christian Story differs here from many another worldview in its sobriety and realism.

DEATH

Human Nature

According to Martin Luther, the will of the human race is curved in toward itself. This "shutupness," to use Kierkegaard's term, wreaks havoc on creation. A twisted will is bent on destruction. Torn apart are the ties that bind. All the relationships of mutuality intended by God are severed. This separation is *death:* "The wages of sin is death" (Rom. 6:23). When we turn from the Light, we are in the Night.

Death in the Story is portrayed as the eviction of Adam and Eve from Paradise:

> Therefore the Lord God sent him forth from the garden of Eden . . . and at the east of the garden of Eden he placed the cherubim, and a sword flaming and turning to guard the way to the tree of life. (Gen. 3:23-24)

The "life" that was intended for humanity is denied to it. It is not blessed with infinite existence in the glorious world of Shalom but cursed with sweat and suffering (Gen. 3:16-19) and "thorns and thistles" (Gen. 3:18). And mortal decay: "You are dust, and to dust you shall return" (Gen. 3:19).

The death-dealing consequences are soon evident in Cain's slaughter of Abel. So much so that soon thereafter

> The Lord was sorry that he had made humankind on the earth, and it grieved him to his heart. (Gen. 6:6)

The broken relationships that came in the wake of sin included the very loss of our contact with God. Thus "the inclination of the human heart is evil from youth" (Gen. 8:21). Knowing good and evil is not knowing God. Thus the loss of free communication between deity and humanity. The human heart is divided against itself as well as separated from God and others.

Things have come to a sad pass for the human race in this chapter of the Story. And the same is so for nature and supernature.

Nature

I think that I shall never see
a poem as lovely as a tree

The eye of the artist perceives beauty in trees. But a greedy glance at the same scene may mean one sees only . . . lumber. As much as the Fall of humans impacts nature, it is also beset by destructive processes in its own life. The same tree extolled by the poet can be attacked by the gypsy moth and struck by lightning. And in some of its forms the earth's growth will itself feed parasitically on life, natural and human.

Such devastation in nature can be written off as part of the cycle of life itself. But the Story wants better things for the tree and the flower. Nature has fallen too, the Story points out. Thus the serpent that seduces and strikes. Thus the fire and flood that throughout do their hurtful work. Thus the desert that is an enemy. And it all could be otherwise: as in its paradisiacal beginnings, so also at the end, God wills flourishing trees and fertile fields, wolves that lie down with lambs, serpents that do not bruise heels but are held in children's hands. God always and everywhere wills Shalom.

Even the lovers of nature cannot, finally, romanticize nature when faced with the cancer cell that fells the seven-year-old and the volcanic ash that pollutes a vast coastal area. We can blame humans for an ozone layer penetrated by our gases and forests destroyed by our acid rain. But we can't make that case for an earthquake that slides a city into the ocean or a flood that wipes out a region's food supply. Yes, the whole creation does groan in travail (Rom. 8:22, RSV). The earth is in pain looking for a new birth, just as is humanity.

What is this "fall" of nature? Tradition associates it with Adam's sin. But how then do we explain the wily serpent's seduction that precedes the human fall? Here again we face "when and where" questions which invite, at the very least, modesty, and at the most, silence. That nature has somehow, somewhere, gone the same way as human nature is right there in the Drama.

Supernature

As we noted, the world of the Story is populated with "principalities and powers" as well as persons and the creatures of nature. Angelic becomes demonic. The orders of creation — their institutions, associations, and organizations that were born to serve — become slaves to sin. And the mysterious "More" of the supernatural world does its devilish work.

"Fantasy and foolishness," says our confident secularity. Still, oddly, our young see on TV and movie screens a regular fare of ghosts and ghouls. And speculation is rife about extra-terrestrial visitors from outer space and extra-temporal messengers from the dead. If these are believable from cultures pop to counter, why not biblical powers that are mysterious and more? These latter are to be numbered as well in the phalanx of foes set against God's purposes.[1] At the very least, we need to capitalize the "e" of this Evil; at most, begin the word with a "D."

---

1. Cf. *The Christian Story*, rev. ed. (Grand Rapids: Wm. B. Eerdmans, 1984), pp. 77-86.

From the Fall there is a rise. But for us and the rest of creation, not yet. More of the Drama is still to come.

QUESTIONS TO CONSIDER

1. Karl Menninger, a famous psychiatrist, recently wrote a book entitled *Whatever Became of Sin?* Well, what did become of it?

2. It has been said that the Christian doctrine of the Fall underlies the "separation of powers" (legislative, executive, and judicial) in the American Constitution. Why would that be so? What do you think about this idea?

3. What are some popular philosophies that disagree with the Christian belief in sin? What are the consequences in attitude and behavior of belief or non-belief in the universality of sin?

4. Some say that the sharp polarization in religion and politics between the armies of Night and the legions of Light — us and them — comes from our failure to take sin seriously in ourselves and our cause as well as in our foes. What do you think?

5. Does the Christian faith make sense without a chapter on the Fall?

6. How do you sort out the issues of What, When, and Where in the biblical story of the Fall?

7. Does nature also participate somehow in the Fall? What implication does our answer have for the "problem of evil," especially natural evil — from cancer cells to earthquakes?

III

Covenant

Is God going to give up on us? No! The good Lord is just getting started.

It did seem to be all downhill after the Fall. Cain killed Abel, the generations came and went, and the text tells us:

> The Lord saw that the wickedness of humankind was great in the earth. . . . And the Lord was sorry that he had made humankind on the earth. (Gen. 6:5-6)

So came the Flood. The many tales of rising water in ancient literature find their counterpart in the Bible. Here the Flood is interpreted as God's way of cleaning up the mess we made. The lesson is this: Judgment follows sin as night follows day.

NOAH

But at the center of the catastrophe is something else. The good God is working out the good Purpose. Thus the deluge sets the stage for the entrance of Noah, who "found favor in the sight of the Lord" (Gen. 6:8). Noah's family and representatives of all living things survive the winds and the waves. And in the heavens appears the rainbow sign. The Bible describes it this way:

> Then God said to Noah and to his sons with him, "As for me, I am establishing my covenant with you . . . and with every living creature that is with you. . . . This is the sign of the covenant that I make between me and you and every living creature that is with you, for all future generations: I have set my bow in the clouds, and it shall be a sign of the covenant between me and the earth." (Gen. 9:8-10, 12-13)

Here is the beginning of a new chapter in the Story. God pledges to stick with the world in spite of its waywardness! That's what a *covenant* is: a promise to be faithful through thick and thin.

But this covenant *gift* carries with it a powerful *demand:* "I'm going to do this with you and for you. Now you be faithful in return." Covenant is a two-way street. So after the rainbow promise come the expectations: Take care of the earth, honor the dignity of every human being, don't shed blood, and so on (Gen. 9:1-7). And underneath all these moral laws lies the command to love and obey God.

What we have here is the *Noachic* covenant, God's promise to give the world enough light and power to make and keep life liveable. God will supply both a *universal* grace to keep the Story going forward and a "general revelation."

The rainbow sign becomes a symbol of God's watch-care of Creation. Here is a Love that won't let us go! This tender mercy over all God's works is *Providence*. Providence means that the everlasting arms are underneath all the world. We see Providence in the regularity and beauty of nature, and in our human capacity to grasp something of the true and the good and to stumblingly seek to do it. So in this fallen world God has still "not left himself without a witness" (Acts 14:17).

Part of God's continuing care is the providential role of civilizing structures. After the Fall, the "orders of creation" become the "orders of preservation." Marriage and the family, the state, the just provision of food, clothing, and shelter — these are ways in which humanity's lethal impulses are kept in check. And more, these institutions are Providence's way of making life liveable and keeping the Story going forward to its purposed end.

But there is more to Providence than the care of the earth and the custody of creation. Providence is *personal* too. So the psalmist cries,

> O Lord, you have searched me and known me . . . and are acquainted with all my ways. (Ps. 139:1, 3)

And Christ offers this word about the divine care:

> Even the hairs of your head are all counted. (Luke 12:7)

We shall meet Providence throughout the Story, a watch-care that is both personal and public, the tender mercies that are over all God's works.

ISRAEL

The plot thickens. God makes another move and another promise — this time closer up and closer in. The Story pinpoints a place and a people: the fertile crescent on the Mediterranean Sea, the people of *Abraham* . . . and Sarah:

> You only have I known of all the families of the earth.
> (Amos 3:2)

"Knowing" in the Bible has the ring of sexual union, of the deepest intimacy. The people of Israel are the *chosen* ones. Of course, God didn't forget the rest of the world. But the Noachic promise not to desert us in the storms of our rebellion still results only in a stalemate. We need a breakthrough. Here it is — the *special* bonding with Israel. (Some call it the doctrine of "Israelology.")

As with Noah, so with Abraham. Promise means *covenant.* God will go through thick and thin with Israel. To what end? Through this chosen people the whole world will be blessed. God will turn the world around! So the chosen people — the special covenant people — are called to rejoice, trust God, and live out their vocation.

Abraham did. He trusted God, and that "faith was reckoned to Abraham as righteousness" (Rom. 4:9). He and Sarah had faith that even in their old age they might have an heir to carry forward the line, as unthinkable, even laughable, as that was (Gen. 18:13; Heb. 11:11). Furthermore, "By faith Abraham . . . set out, not knowing where he was going" (Heb. 11:8).

God's history with Israel continues through many ups and downs. And at the center of this life together comes a covenantal deed to which both Jews and Christians look with awe: God's new bonding with this people through the covenant with *Moses:*

> I am the Lord your God, who brought you out of the land of Egypt, out of the house of slavery. (Exod. 20:2)

So comes *another* act of God, confirming the original call to Abraham. The promise to watch over Israel takes shape as a release of this particular people of God from Egyptian captivity. A baby in the bullrushes is raised up (*"grace"!*) to lead a nation to a land flowing with milk and honey.

The God of *liberation* continues now as the God of *expectation*. After the indicative comes the imperative: "I am the Lord your God"; *therefore:*

> You shall have no other gods before me. You shall not make for yourself an idol. . . . You shall not murder. You shall not commit adultery. You shall not steal. (Exod. 20:2-4, 13-15)

The covenant-God is a "therefore God." The first expectation is that we trust God, not something else — the *first table* of the Ten Commandments, with its call to us to love God with all our heart, soul, and mind. The next expectation is the *second table* of the Ten Commandments — to love our neighbor.

What is all this other than the original vision? From the beginning, the world God wills is one in which we have a life together with God and with one another. Here it is, all over again — the same vision of the reign of God that has been buried deeply in the human heart but obscured by sin. Now it's out in the open. This people will always know what God expects with unparalleled clarity. Israel is a "light to the nations" in many ways. One of the ways in which they shed this light is through their knowledge of the law and the prophets and thus their role as the conscience of the human community.

The patience of God persists. The ups and downs continue. Kings rise and fall; prophets sound the call and are silenced; priests come and go. Through it all, Israel, like the rest of us, tests that patience of the "long-suffering" God. So covenant judgment follows covenant call: "You only have I known of all the families of the earth; therefore I will punish you for all your iniquities" (Amos 3:2). Yet an amazing grace continues.

Prophets and priests play an important role in Israel's journey. A prophet is a *forthteller* of God's patience and fortitude. The prophet delivers a forthright word from God. Usually it is a reminder of things forgotten: Here is the gift you received, and here is the promise you made. Do what you promised!

Do it and *see* it. Do it because you see it . . . out ahead, the Dream of God, Shalom. The prophet is also a pointer to the future, a *foreteller* as well as a forthteller. The prophet's finger aims at God's intended realm of righteousness — the coming time of truth, faith, justice, peace. "Go for it!"

But the future is a *promise* as well as a plea. God *will* bring such a world — a wonder-filled time and place when swords will be beaten into plowshares, spears into pruning hooks (Isa. 2:4), where each will eat from his or her own vine and fig tree (Isa. 36:16), where even the wolf and the lamb will lie down together and the child will put its hand over the snake's hole (Isa. 11:6-9). All the broken bonds that mar our world will be healed, every flaw mended — the promise of a dream come true.

This can be very intimidating. Prophets can be real nuisances. We shut them up. Visions of things to come and things to do? No, thank you! We stone prophets.

Enter the priest. Priests make sacrifices. Why? To fend off the punishment so richly deserved by people who stone prophets.

Whether these sacrifices work is another question. As ancient (and modern) religions had their prophets, so too they had their priests with offerings aplenty, from grain and animals to money and human life.

Israel's priests had their altars also. Sin needs to be forgiven. The long-suffering God is a merciful God. But for
them *penitence* is better than *payments:*

> The sacrifice acceptable to God is a broken spirit; a broken and
> contrite heart, O God, you will not despise. (Ps. 51:17)

Coming on stage, in addition to the *prophet* Isaiah and
the *priest* Aaron, is *King* David. In a fallen world, we need a
power to sustain our life together, to rule over — indeed, to
overrule — the passions that make for pains in the body
politic. We need governance, a model of what a holy com-
monwealth might be like. Thus the royal Davidic covenant,
a sign and a hope for a holy nation.

Prophetic, priestly, and *royal* signs of God's Hope! "Por-
tents" of things to come. Isaiah dreamed of the coming together of these ministries in one whom he described this way:

> He had no form or majesty that we should look at him, nothing
> in his appearance that we should desire him. He was despised
> and rejected by others; a man of suffering and acquainted with
> infirmity. . . . Surely he has borne our infirmities and carried
> our diseases; yet we accounted him stricken, struck down by
> God, and afflicted. But he was wounded for our transgressions,
> crushed for our iniquities; upon him was the punishment that
> made us whole, and by his bruises we are healed. (Isa. 53:2-5)

As Christians we read these words through our own
special lens: this is a description of Christ, our unique prophet,
priest, and king. That's an important part of the next chapter
of the Story. But Jews also believe that the narrative goes on.
Their hopes for the future could be the coming of a Messianic
deliverer, in history or beyond it, or the fulfillment of Shalom

in this world or the next — in the land of their forebears, or in all the cosmos. Christians share with Jews the final cosmic hope that God will be all and in all. But in the Christian Story the End already makes its entrance in the One who has borne our griefs and carried our sorrows.[1]

CONTINUING COVENANT WITH ISRAEL

The covenant with Noah continues to the end of time. So too does God's bonding with Israel:

> The gifts and the calling of God are irrevocable. (Rom. 11:29)

The gifts given include the vision of Shalom, the solidarity of God with the people chosen to see it, and the grace to trust the covenant-Maker. The calling is to serve the vision seen, to keep company with the ever-present God, and to seize the faith offered. As the custodian of "the law and the prophets," Israel is the conscience of the human community. Since they are the people with whom God has special dealings, and into whose very midst God comes to embody Shalom and to reconcile the world to that Purpose in Jesus Christ, their covenant is "irrevocable."

The permanence of Israel's covenant has been a puzzle to many Christians. It seems to conflict with the *new* covenant in Jesus Christ: Do we need the Old when we have the New?

The belief that Israel's covenant has been abrogated ("supersessionism") has been sincerely held by countless Christians, without much thought about the New Testament's

---

1. Cf. *The Christian Story*, rev. ed. (Grand Rapids: Wm. B. Eerdmans, 1984), pp. 87-96.

own struggle with the issue, and without much awareness of the consequences that this replacement theory can have. One of those consequences has been the fueling of the fires of hate. "Jews are Christ-killers!" screams the white-sheeted Klan preacher. The results are burning crosses and broken synagogue windows — and much worse, for such accusations have resulted in the villifying and terrorizing of Jews throughout Christian history. Although the Holocaust happened in a country taken over by a pagan philosophy, it arose in a nation with a long Christian tradition. Thus anti-Judaism can prepare the soil for the seeds of anti-Semitism. The continuing pogroms and persecutions are pressing Christians to go back to their biblical charter and rethink some of the inherited teaching about the theology of Christians and Jews.

Here, as elsewhere in our Story, we are faced with conflicting views. Those at the extremes are often the most vocal. Some argue that *any* claim that Christ is special — Lord and Savior of all — automatically results in the persecution of Jews and therefore has to be dropped. Others say that God replaced Israel's covenant with the church, and has been punishing the Jews ever since for rejecting Christ. While these extremes have been repudiated by most Christians, there is still no "ecumenical consensus" on the matter. But there is a growing number of church statements which question the teaching that the covenant with Israel has been abrogated. These statements try to say *both* that God's bond with Israel is irrevocable *and* that God's special coming in Christ reconciled the whole world.[2] *How* that could be is left

2. See *The Theology of the Churches and the Jewish People: Statements by the World Council of Churches and Its Member Churches* (Geneva: WCC Publications, 1988).

up in the air, since there is still no clear "mind of the church." Here we affirm the paradox found in Paul's deep struggle with this matter in chapters 9 through 11 in his letter to the Romans. On the one hand, the Jewish people's "gifts and calling are irrevocable." Indeed, "all Israel will be saved" (Rom. 11:26)! On the other hand, to *all* comes the Word: "If you confess with your lips that Jesus is Lord and believe in your heart that God raised him from the dead, you will be saved" (Rom. 10:9).

Because of the honor that Christian believers give to Israel, they will fight against anti-Semitism and anti-Judaism wherever they rear their ugly heads. And they will join with their spiritual kin in a common struggle toward Shalom. But because they also believe in the next chapter of the Story, they will not exclude their spiritual kin from hearing about the coming of the One in whom they so profoundly trust.

It is from Jews that Christians have learned to yearn for the embodiment of Shalom. And we have been taught as well to expect its coming. So we arrive at the center of the Christian Story: Jesus Christ. "He is our peace" — our Shalom.

QUESTIONS TO CONSIDER

1. What are some of the universal laws of life that are part of the covenant with Noah and "general revelation"?

2. Does a belief in the covenant with Noah have any implications for how much people of different religions and philosophies of life can talk about and even agree on moral issues and public policy?

3. What would the Bible be without its inclusion of the Hebrew Scriptures? Is the second-century "Marcionism" that rejected the Old Testament and polarized the God of Israel and the God of Jesus still around?

4. What does Shalom mean?

5. What can we learn from the prophets? The priests? The kings?

6. Does the covenant of God with Israel continue to this day? Think about the issues of "supersessionism" and "anti-supersessionism" and examine the church statements on the subject.

Jesus Christ

"Prepare to meet thy God!" shouts the billboard of the new interdenominational chapel on the outskirts of town. That should sober us all as we think about meeting our Maker. But something's wrong here. We don't have to wait until the End for that. We've *already* met! That's what this chapter is about. Jesus Christ is "the human face of God."

This meeting was a long time coming, so the Story goes: from the mists of our beginnings, through the cataclysmic Fall, through the rainbow promise, to Israel's covenant. "*How* long, O Lord?"

A time did come, as the carol tells it, when "the hopes and fears of all the years [were] met in him tonight." God *met* us firsthand. The silence ended with the Word spoken. Indeed, "the Word became flesh and lived among us" (John 1:14)!

Just what meeting God in the flesh means is the subject of "Christology," the *doctrine of Christ.* Our earlier line drawing shows us the link between this chapter and the preceding ones:

The God who is Life Together brings creation into being for that purpose:

But then comes the "No!" to God's "Yes":

God refuses to take "No!" for an answer and makes the rainbow promise:

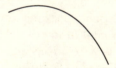

Then God makes the special covenant with Israel:

And now God makes his own entry into the world:

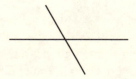

Christian Basics

These last lines represent the church's ancient teaching about Jesus Christ. The line of God intersects our line below — this symbolizes the enfleshment of God, *Incarnation*. The lines also make a cross. God and the world have become at one . . . at-one-ment. *Atonement*. Here are the two sides of the doctrine of Christ. Incarnation tells us about the "Person" — *who* Christ is. And the Atonement tells us about the "Work" — *what* Christ did to make us one with God.

THE PERSON: INCARNATION

Truly God

Who *is* Jesus Christ? He is "the only Son from the Father" (John 1:14, RSV). John's reply takes us back into eternity itself. This Galilean carpenter is somehow united to the inner being of God — a parental union of the Persons.

To put it John's way: God speaks a Word. But God's Word did not just happen — it always was! "In the beginning was the Word, and the Word was with God, and the Word *was* God" (John 1:1, italics added). The Word is God's eternal Purpose: Jesus Christ. God with the Word, the Father with the Son, the Purposer with the Purpose — forever together. Christ eternal, truly God.

We are back to the *Trinity*. As the Word that always was with God, the eternal Christ is a Person within the triune Being. And more! Christ is always in God's Doing as well, active wherever God is at work in the Story — "pre-existing" in creation and covenant, and now incarnate in Jesus of Nazareth. So the eternal Son, Jesus Christ, shares in the

40

divine Life Together with the Father and the Spirit — Purpose, Purposer, Power — truly God:

And as truly God, Jesus Christ — Purpose-in-action — is there in every chapter of the Story:

Only such a Person can do the Work of overcoming alienation and bringing reconciliation.

Truly Human

A babe in a manger and a carpenter at a bench — God? God in the disguise of a human? "Yes" to the first, "No" to the second. *No* disguise, because Jesus was truly *human*. When his stomach was empty, he hungered; when his throat was parched, he thirsted. He bled when cut; he needed sleep, clothing, and shelter. His mind and body developed like yours and mine: he "increased in wisdom and in stature" (Luke 2:52, RSV). His spirit, as well as his mind and body, had its vicissitudes, for he was "tested as we are" (Heb. 4:15). Here was a human being, not a god walking around the earth playing make-believe. And the ultimate sign of Jesus' humanness was the horrible death he died on the cross.

So Jesus Christ is right there on the horizontal plane along with the rest of us, intersecting it:

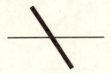

How could it be otherwise with the God who stoops to conquer? The struggle to liberate us from sin, death, and evil, which have taken us captive, has to be fought where these powers dwell — right in our midst. The long-suffering God does not operate from the top down, by fiat, but meets us where we live, chooses to be in solidarity with all that we are. Jesus Christ, "the Word made *flesh*" — truly human.

Rightly Human

When getting that Story straight, we have to be clear about *what kind* of a human being Jesus was. Yes, he was "tested as we are" — "yet," the writer adds, "without sin" (Heb. 4:15). If Jesus was true to God's purpose, then he was turned to the Light, not the Night. The miracle of his coming is that he was what we are supposed to be — true to God, a *true* human being in that sense as well. This "sinlessness" means having unclouded vision and moving in the right direction — toward God and toward the neighbor in need — being "*rightly* human." So Jesus was human in *every* sense: what we *are* in our weakness, and also what we *ought* to be.

"Born of the Virgin Mary"

When God comes among us, there is *Power* with the Purpose — the dynamism of the Holy Spirit. Something dramatic is bound to take place, a manifestation of Deity's presence. In the ancient church, the virginal conception of Jesus was just such a sign. It still stands for the fact that the Power of God brought into being the Purpose of God.

But we've learned that to believe in "the virgin birth" is no guarantee that one really holds Jesus to be "truly God." The early Adoptionists were quite definite about it, but they denied the deity of Christ. And it could well be that for people today the most potent evidence of the work of the Spirit in Jesus is the Shalom incarnate in his life, death, and resurrection.

Mary's appearance in Scripture, in the creeds of the church, and in the piety of many believers is a tribute to her importance in the Story. While a protest against an exaggerated role for her was in order, it's been too easy to go to the other extreme and ignore her place in the scheme of things. Today, women in the church searching for points of contact in the tradition have discovered her as a role model. Indeed, she was the first believer! And "Mary's song" is a powerful witness to the kind of God with whom we have to do in Jesus:

> He has brought down the powerful from their thrones,
> and lifted up the lowly;
> he has filled the hungry with good things,
> and sent the rich away empty. (Luke 1:52-53)

Truly One

Whatever comes from God bears the stamp of God's nature. Therefore, the *togetherness* of the triune God (Prologue) is reflected in the unity of Christ's Person. There is no "separation" of the "two natures," as the Chalcedon Definition puts it. Jesus is *one* Person.

What we have here defies logic. We need *both* intersecting lines in our diagram — God above *and* humanity below. "Jesus Christ, truly God, truly human, and truly one," as the early church said. Actually, it took the church four hundred years to put it this way. Here it is in the famous words of the Council of Chalcedon in 451:

> Our Lord Jesus Christ, perfect in Godhead, perfect in Manhood, very God and very Man . . . in two natures, without confusion, without change, without division, without separation, one Person not parted or divided into two persons, but the one and the same Son, only begotten God-Logos. . . .

This was a hard-won formula. For a long time the church had to contend with polarized positions, half-truths or "heresies." One side stressed the humanity of Christ, and the other stressed the deity. The parties of the Ebionites, the Adoptionists, the Arians, and the Nestorians were in the former camp. And the Docetists, the Modalists, the Apollinarians, and the Monophysites in the same eras represented the other. We still have these factions! It's either *The Last Temptation of Christ* on one side, or the folk who picket the film on the other. The film portrays Jesus as a human being — period. The opposition says that he was God walking around as a make-believe human. But the Story tells us Jesus was both divine and human. And so the church has said since.

We have run into a "paradox." We will find them all over the Story. A *theological* paradox holds together two seemingly contradictory points. Here is the paradox in this case: Jesus is *both* fully human and fully divine, in inseparable unity. If we don't hang on to this, sooner or later something basic gets lost from the biblical picture of Christ. And the same thing is true about other mysteries of faith that we'll meet: the church as *both* the Body of Christ and a human body of people, salvation as *both* by grace and by our human decisions — the former working through the latter. We can *explore* these mysteries, but we can't *explain* them. So we live by faith on this shadowside of the journey. Someday we shall see in the Light (1 Cor. 13:12)!

THE WORK: ATONEMENT

We come now to a crucial turn in the Story. What happens here determines its outcome. Christians believe that the broken bonds were mended. Those at enmity were made at one. At-one-ment. Atonement! Here is a very special word in the church's vocabulary. It means that God put things together again in the deed Christ did. "Salvation" happened.

"In Christ, God was reconciling . . ." (2 Cor. 5:19). By this decisive deed we were liberated from the things that separate us from one another . . . and One another. Reconciliation!

Precisely because atonement is so important, feelings run high about what it means. Let's tune in on the long conversation in the church and listen to different points of view.

Jesus as Example and Teacher

This view stresses Jesus as a Galilean teacher who went about doing good. He taught about the Kingdom of God, and he practiced what he preached. His simple message was that we are to love God and love our neighbor. The Sermon on the Mount says it all.

The "Work" of Jesus is to get rid of the things in our life that prevent us from right living. We need to have our ignorance about love cleared up and our apathy challenged. That's what a good teaching example does. Jesus was the perfect one. Hence this school of thought stresses Jesus' example and is therefore called "exemplarism." It doesn't often use the word "atonement," but it does tell us how to "at-one" with God and the world around us: follow the example of Jesus and obey his moral and spiritual teachings.

How could Christian basics *not* include these things? Impossible. Jesus *is* our example and teacher. He reveals the God of love and the love of God. And Jesus calls us to follow him through thick and thin in the service of our neighbor in need.

Many Christians who have tried this theory say it goes far, but *not far enough.* "Trying it" here means practicing it with passion. For example, for just one day, follow the directives in the Sermon on the Mount *without compromise:* go the second mile, turn the other cheek when struck, give up cloak as well as coat, as Jesus did and as he taught (Matt. 5:38-42). When we really try, we soon find out how self-centered we are, and how far short we fall of these standards. There's a message here. We find out something about ourselves.

And we learn something else about Jesus. He's more than a law-giver. One sensitive soul, laboring under the burden of a religion whose only word was "follow Jesus," put it this way: "I don't need good advice. I need good news!"

That's just what the Gospel is — Good News! . . . the glad tidings that God loves us even when we *don't* measure up. Following Jesus means heeding the wonderful News that "my yoke is easy, and my burden is *light*" (Matt. 11:30, italics added). The Work of Christ must have something to do with people like Paul who cry out,

> I do not do the good I want, but the evil I do not want is what I do. (Rom. 7:19)

The Gospel is *more* than a burdensome "should." It is a sheer gift — "grace," as the Bible calls it.

And there is even more. The Gospel is Good News for *sufferers* as well as sinners. "There *is* a balm in Gilead," as the gospel song puts it. The Work of Christ is "liberation" — from suffering and the foes that inflict it, and from our final enemy, death.

This first view makes an important point. But it also leaves out something basic.

Jesus as Substitute and Savior

This second theory specializes in news for a fallen world: "Christ died for your sins!" "Believe in the Lord Jesus and you will be saved!" Its advocates find the Gospel at the foot of the cross — on Calvary more than in Galilee. They don't hesitate to use the word "atonement." After all, it comes from the ancient practice of altar sacrifice.

The reason for the blood, the sacrifice, the death is Sin. The human problem is our rebellion against God — not the

47

need for knowledge of the good. Since Adam and Eve, we have all broken the law of God. But, says this view, we aren't going to get away with it. Guilt will be punished, *eternally*.

But something remarkable happened with the coming of Christ. And it happened on the cross. Right then and there, Jesus took the sentence of death we deserve. He could take our place because he was a human being. And, because he was divine at the same time, his suffering had eternal value, substituting for the eternal punishment we were due. As a result, God accepted Jesus' death as payment for our crime. We are saved on Calvary from the wrath of God.

This view is powerful. It "preaches well." It had a big impact in the history of missions, and it thrives today in movements of mass evangelism. Its influence can also be seen in the altars of Christendom that represent Christ's sacrifice and the broken body and shed blood of holy communion.

In its long and broad history, this view has come in different forms. Jesus' substitution has been portrayed in various ways — sometimes as "penal," a sentence imposed by a judge on the accused; sometimes as a priestly sacrifice offered up to Deity; sometimes as paying the price due a prince's offended honor.

How can we *not* say that Jesus died for us? The cross *is* at the heart of the Gospel! There is no Good News if it is not Good News for sinners. We *are* saved by faith in the Work of Christ on Calvary. But there is more to it than this.

The *more* is suggested by the conclusion drawn by a convert who was taught that the blood of Jesus satisfied the justice of God. He said, "I love Jesus, but I hate God."

If Jesus was "down there" on the cross, and God was "up there" in heaven punishing Jesus instead of us, what does this say about God? For one thing, it seems to contradict a key teaching about atonement:

In Christ *God* was reconciling the world. . . . (2 Cor. 5:19)

God was not up in heaven while Jesus was down on earth. God was right there *in* Jesus! We have just seen that the *In*carnation is a basic Christian belief: Jesus Christ is truly God as well as truly human. God as the "second Person of the Trinity" is somehow bound up with everything experienced by the human Jesus right "down there" on Calvary.

Speaking of the Trinity, we saw in the Prologue that the three Persons are utterly together, so we can't polarize the Father and Son any more than we can separate God from Jesus.

Missing from the substitution view is a point made by the exemplarist view: God is, through and through, a God of love. God is *so* loving that the divine heart itself breaks on Calvary. In Jesus, *God* took the punishment for us. *Yes,* the holiness of God does judge sin. Here the proponents of the substitution view are right. It's *tough* love we're talking about — not *sloppy* Agape! When we turn from the Light, we're in the Night. But the miracle of the cross is that this judgment of God falls in Jesus on . . . *God!* The *Judge* is judged. The suffering of Jesus is also the pain of God. Jesus' cry of abandonment on the cross is God's own lament.

Our second view teaches a deep truth. But it also leaves out something basic.

Jesus as Lord and Liberator

A third view accents Jesus' *triumph.* Taking its cue from the ruling power of ancient potentates, this "victor" view focuses on "Lordship." The key to the Work of Christ becomes the *resurrection* more than the life and teaching of Jesus (view 1) or the crucifixion (view 2). As the Easter song goes, "Up from the grave he arose, with a mighty triumph o'er his foes!" The last enemy to fall was *death*. And *all* the "authorities and rulers," the principalities and powers of evil, as well as death, met their match in Jesus the conqueror.

Adherents of this view believe our basic problem in life is the misery caused by these powers. Jesus overcame them all and released those held in their bondage. Jesus, Lord and Liberator!

The advocates of this view have been many and varied. In the early centuries, the foes were Satan and his minions. Some of the church fathers pictured the fray as a fishing expedition in which Christ in his purity was the bait let down on the hook of God, enticing the Devil to lunge for him . . . and get caught! In later centuries when the church was under fire or the world was under the heel of a tyrant, it was Christ the Victor who consoled and empowered. Currently, liberation theologies march into the battle against oppression under the banner of "Christ the Liberator."

How can the resurrection *not* be at the heart of Good News? Easter is inseparable from Good Friday. The Gospel calls us to "resist the powers of evil." We do so in the confidence that they have *already* been defeated by the risen Christ. But surely there is more.

This *more* has to do with the way the victor view interprets evil. It sees the enemy as "out there." So it is. But what of the "enemy within"? Life is not a battle in which the armies of Light are drawn up against the legions of Night. Sin is active in *all* camps, afflicting the champions of justice as well as its foes. Christ *is* a Lord who gives us hope in the struggle against evil. But he is also a Savior *from the sin in ourselves.* So *faith* in the Work on Calvary must join *hope* in the Easter victory.

And *love* joins both. The loving God at the forefront in the exemplarist view challenges the militaristic tenor of the victor view. The victory is won by *vulnerability.* The weapon of liberation is crucifixion. Jesus Christ reigns from the cross! The power of God, the Lordship of Christ, is *powerlessness.* The ways of God are not the ways of the world. How this works out in the life of the Christian we must yet struggle with in Chapter VI.

Our third view teaches a deep truth. But it leaves out something basic.

Jesus as Presence

According to the fourth view, *God* is the atoning Actor. The very coming of God into our midst is the act of reconciliation. Incarnation *is* Atonement.

The human problem, according to the presence view, is the quick passage of life. The mind of the ancients often contemplated with sadness the fleeting character of time; the things we love never last. But the eye of faith sees the world differently. The Word became flesh, and changed the destiny of this passing world from death to life. Mortality was transformed into immortality. By the sheer presence of God, the Incarnation, this vale of darkness and death was given Light and Life. *Bethlehem* makes the world at one with God.

How can it *not* be that the coming of Eternity into time changes everything? The Incarnation makes all the difference in the world. But there *is* something more. The "more" is God's dealing with the foes that meet us right here in time — sin, evil, and error. Incarnation is *for the purpose of* Atonement. Without the Power of God to confront these powers, there is "no contest." The Story depends on this Presence. Incarnation is necessary to Christ's work, but Incarnation is not its limit. It makes possible the continuing tasks of the Galilean teacher who rescues us from untruth, the Calvary savior who delivers us from sin, and the Easter liberator who overcomes suffering and death.

* * *

We have been rendering the discussion of the Work of Christ in sharp lines and distinct theories. Of course, life is never this neat. Sometimes views are found in combination or are missing one or another feature we have mentioned. Nevertheless, the four views discussed are four *tendencies* that assert themselves. There *is* another view to which we shall presently turn. But it is important to know the conversation that has gone on in the church. And the insights of each of the views examined make their contribution to a fuller view that has developed in the church. In the following chart we list the features of each view under the points we have covered: the *issue* that it addresses, the *locus* in Jesus' career that it stresses, the *focus* on what is changed, the *action* performed by Christ, and the *outcome*.

Model	Issue	Locus	Focus	Action	Outcome
Example and Teacher	ignorance and apathy	Galilee	Human attitudes and behavior	disclosure by word and deed of love of God and neighbor	illumination and inspiration
Substitute and Savior	sin and guilt	Calvary	relationship of God to humanity	vicarious suffering and death	judgment turned to mercy
Conqueror and Lord	evil and death	Easter	powers and principalities	resurrection victory	defeat of powers of evil and death
Presence	transiency and mortality	Bethlehem	temporality	incarnation	life and immortality

An Inclusive View

Throughout Christian history an understanding of the liberating and reconciling Work of Christ has appeared that takes account of all the stages of Christ's career and the basic insights of each perspective we have examined. Furthermore, it honors the flow of the Story by connecting with the chapter on Covenant, showing Jesus' roots in Israel and its tradition of prophetic, priestly, and royal leaders. Although theologian John Calvin developed in detail this inclusive idea, called the "threefold office of Christ," it is found in the teaching traditions of many churches — Protestant, Roman Catholic, and Eastern Orthodox. It fits especially well the ecumenical approach of *Christian Basics*.

The Prophetic Jesus

What do prophets do? They make things plain, *forthtelling* the truth. The Old Testament prophets called it as they saw it. And they spoke for God, not by their own authority.

Prophets *foretell* as well as forthtell. In Scripture they are "seers" of a vision of the world God willed. They look to the Future that God intends. And they proclaim the promises of God: in the face of all resistance, God would bring a world of Shalom.

Jesus was the Prophet par excellence! He told it like it was, boldly proclaiming the will and the way of God. And he brought news, different news than that of his contemporary, John the Baptist, in the line of the great Hebrew prophets. Not the bad news of fiery judgment but the Good News of reconciliation.

Jesus was a foreteller as well as a forthteller. The news he brought was of a Kingdom coming. The Rule of God was on its way. Rejoice! Shalom was arriving; the righteous realm of God could not be turned aside. In making this announcement, he recalled the words of another prophet:

> The Spirit of the Lord is upon me, because he has anointed me to bring good news to the poor. He has sent me to proclaim release to the captives and recovery of sight to the blind, to let the oppressed go free, to proclaim the year of the Lord's favor. (Luke 4:18-19)

When Jesus finished making this announcement, he said, in effect, "This is it!":

> Today this scripture has been fulfilled in your hearing. (Luke 4:21)

This "today" has even deeper meaning in the message of Jesus. We have not only the preacher of the coming Kingdom but also the *arrival* of God's Rule. The Kingdom was actually *here* as well as near. It had *already* begun in Jesus!

Signs and miracles of its advent abound:

> The blind receive their sight, the lame walk, the lepers are cleansed, the deaf hear, the dead are raised, and the poor have good news brought to them. (Matt. 11:5)

The captive, the sick and sorrowful, the outcast, the sinner finally come home. Every "nobody" touched by Jesus became a "somebody." Shalom broke through! Evil met its match! Jesus said,

> I watched Satan fall from heaven like a flash of lightning. (Luke 10:18)

All this, of course, marked only the beginning. The poor are still with us, the sick cry on beds of pain, the oppressed groan under the heel of the tyrant. We still await "the acceptable year of the Lord." That means the Kingdom is *Not Yet* as well as *Already*. Its first waves have washed up on the shores of time, but its fulfillment is yet to be. But we now wait with hope, trusting the promise of the Prophet.

Meanwhile, we are called to action. Jesus the Seer announced another secret of the Kingdom — the *way* Shalom works: *Agape*. Hope is fulfilled only through love. And this is so because the God of hope *is* Agape (1 John 4:7).

How the divine Agape is expressed through our love is the subject of many of Jesus' injunctions to his followers. They form a rising crescendo: (a) Agape is love of the *neighbor* (Luke 10:25-37). It is having the eyes to see and the hands to serve the victim on the Jericho road, the forgotten and forlorn. (b) Even more, Agape is loving the *lawless* as well as the loveless. Jesus companied with sinners. He consorted with the despised tax collector and adulteress (Matt. 9:11; Luke 5:27; John 8:3-11). (c) And yet more. Agape is loving the *enemy*. Its open arms embrace those who hate and hurt it (Matt. 5:43-44). In this highest form, Agape reveals its unconditional, "no-matter-what" way. It will not be turned aside by any rejection (Luke 15:20). It loves the unlovable and unloving. It turns the other cheek and goes the second mile (Matt. 5:38-44). Utter love, therefore, is *fore*-giving — ready to give before there is any payoff — and forgiving in the face of rebuff. Agape "does not insist on its own way" (1 Cor. 13:5), giving without stint or calculation.

Jesus not only taught Agape; he lived it. Prophets practice what they preach. Jesus welcomed and served the loveless, the lawless, and the enemy:

> Whoever wishes to become great among you must be your servant, and whoever wishes to be first among you must

be slave of all. For the Son of Man came not to be served but to serve, and to give his life a ransom for many. (Mark 10:43-45)

He said it and he did it.

Notice what this kind of loving gets you. Self-giving ends in just that — sacrificing your life, giving it up, dying. Prophets get stoned for their trouble. Jesus was handed a cross. The fallen world does not take kindly to radical love. Agape sears our conscience. We snuff out the flame.

But what happens as a result? Prophets *expose* our condition as well as *disclose* God's intention. We are made to face up to the kind of people we are. We are forced to answer "yes" to the spiritual's painful question, "Were you there when they crucified my Lord?" Indeed, we were right there, ready with hammer and nails.

Prophetic judgment that falls on us is the most painful of all — the fiery elements of spurned Love . . . "burning coals" (Rom. 12:20). How can we find healing? "There *is* a balm in Gilead"! So the Priest joins the Prophet in Christ's at-one-ing Work.

The Priestly Jesus

The priests of Israel offered sacrifices for the sins of the people. The blood of lambs was offered to turn away the judgment of God.

So too Christians believe a sacrifice was made — for the sins of all of us. There was a Priest, and it was Christ. There was a Lamb, and it was Christ as well. So it is sung in the innermost sanctuary of Christian worship, when the bread and wine of Christ's body and blood are shared:

Christ, thou Lamb of God who takes away the sins of the world.

Christians believe the foretelling came true of One about whom Isaiah said,

> He was wounded for our transgressions,
> crushed for our iniquities.
> Upon him was the punishment that made us whole,
> and by his bruises we are healed.
> . . . His life [was] an offering for sin. (Isa. 53:5-6, 10)

But then we wonder, "What kind of business is this? — having the innocent victim take the punishment for a guilty party?" Retribution is bad enough. But when it falls on someone who doesn't deserve it, it's *criminal*.

As we have seen, "substitution" theories of the atonement have been accused of this. But that's because they neglect a significant teaching:

> In Christ, God was reconciling the world. . . . (2 Cor. 5:19)

Calvary's Priest was *God* in Christ. God's tough love was taken by God's merciful love — in Christ. "Satisfaction" was made *by* God as well as *to* God. God was *both* the author *and* the receiver of the sacrificial Work accomplished on the cross.

Does this mean that God *died* for us? That God stopped existing? Impossible. God is *eternal*. Calvary was not the death *of* God but death *in* God! The great heart of God took death into itself. On Calvary, God "died a little death," so to speak. We stammer as we try to say the unsayable. We need the help of the poets and the hymn writers who speak of "the cross in the heart of God," the "crucified God," and the very "blood of God."

What sounds incomprehensible in theological language becomes clear in a story. That's why so many stories appear in Scripture. Imagine, in Jesus' parable of the Prodigal Son, what it cost the father to welcome home that "Number One" offspring (Luke 15:11-32). Oriental fathers have high expectations of their sons and are stern in reproval of their failure. But here was one father who saw his son returning from "wasted substance" and was unaware of his remorse, yet welcomed him still:

> While he was still far off, his father saw him and was filled with compassion; he ran and put his arms around him and kissed him. (Luke 15:20)

What a cauldron of emotions in that parent's soul! What did it take to send him running to meet his son? Something inside, a love so large that it could take into itself righteous indignation and judgment. The text calls it "compassion," an inner suffering in which the tenderness of Agape absorbed its toughness.

God's own suffering love is like that of the waiting and eagerly accepting parent in the parable: On the cross, the love of God takes into itself the wrath of God, as Luther put it. The judgment fell, but it fell upon the Judge. This miracle of Good News is at the heart of our Story. That's why the cross is at the center of our sanctuaries. It announces Jesus Christ—true God, true human—*our Savior*.

The victory of the cross is not hidden in the mists of Golgotha but revealed by the sun of Easter morning. God reigns! "The gates of hell" cannot prevail against God. And so we come to the royal role of Christ.

The Royal Jesus

The resurrection of Jesus Christ changes everything. As Paul forcefully insisted, "If Christ has not been raised, your faith is futile" (1 Cor. 15:17). Christ's royal victory means the prophetic and priestly work have been accomplished: ignorance is over; sin and guilt are no more! *And* all the other foes of God go down to defeat, including "the last enemy," death.

In the Bible there is a militancy to the Easter message:

> [God] raised him from the dead. . . . He disarmed the rulers and authorities and made a public example of them, triumphing over them in it. (Col. 2:12, 15)

And this militancy is connected with royalty:

> God put this power to work in Christ when he raised him from the dead and seated him at his right hand in the heavenly places, far above all rule and authority and power and dominion, and above every name that is named, not only in this age but also in the age to come. (Eph. 1:20-21)

Today we might call such a victory "liberation." Jesus frees the world from all the swashbuckling "powers and principalities" that imperil Shalom. Such "rulers and authorities" — designated by God for a good end, as we saw in Chapter I — have gone astray. But we no longer fear them. Storm and rage they may, but they don't run things anymore. John Milton expressed this eloquently in his poem entitled "On the Morning of Christ's Nativity":

> That old Dragon underground
> in straighter limits bound,
> Not half so far casts his usurped sway
> and wroth to see his Kingdom fail,
> Swings the scaly horror of his folded tail.

While the End is Not Yet and the tail of the dragon can still do us harm, it cannot prevail. Jesus Christ is *Lord and Liberator*.

The Risen Jesus

What actually happened to Jesus on Easter morning? Theories abound. In our day some try to explain it in terms acceptable to the modern mind. Consider a few such ideas: (1) Jesus' resurrection was a hallucination or fantasy. The disciples wanted it to happen so badly that they dreamed it up. (2) No, the disciples didn't dream Jesus' resurrection or fake it; they really did *feel* it. They experienced a new assurance, somehow, somewhere. Without that surge of new hope, the Christian religion would never have gotten started. But we can't say it happened as described, with the real Jesus and an empty tomb. (3) Psychically speaking, lots of strange things happen. Why not with Jesus — great prophet that he was? Just as the dead sometimes return to give us messages, so this great Mystic came from the other world and reappeared to his followers. And the theories go on and on. . . .

We face some hard choices here. We can and do try to fit the resurrection — and other events in Jesus' life — into the limits of our experience. But there is a problem: the second chapter of the Story. As sinners, we don't want anyone telling us what to do. So, in the case of Jesus, why not make him fit into our theories and scale of things? A truly risen Lord who disarms all the powers and principalities and claims total allegiance, including our own, is very threatening. So let's tame the terror and deny that it really happened.

Or we can let the claims stand as they are — embarrassing, disorienting, overwhelming . . . an "offense" and a "stumbling-block," as Scripture describes them.

We accept the royal claims as presented in Scripture. And they lead us back to this chapter's refrain in the Story: the Work is done by the Person. And the Person is truly

61

God as well as truly human. This means that God's mighty deed in this royal office cannot be squeezed into our pint-size human containers. God bursts all our boundaries. This real human being, Jesus, was raised from the dead by the Power of God.

Not just part of Jesus but all of him was in solidarity with us in suffering and death. And not just part of him but all of him rose on Easter. This means that we look with hope at the End for the "resurrection of the body." It means that we embrace the demand to honor the body and fight for those deprived of its basic needs — food, clothing, and shelter. And it means that we share in his victory:

> Christ has been raised from the dead, the first fruits of those who have died. . . . Death has been swallowed up in victory. . . . Thanks be to God, who gives us the victory through our Lord Jesus Christ. (1 Cor. 15:20, 54, 57)

*   *   *

Christians believe that they *have* met their Maker. They see the human face of God in Jesus Christ. Just so, the *Incarnation*, the Person truly human, truly divine, truly one. So also the *Atonement*, the *prophetic*, *priestly*, and *royal* Work done in the life, death, and resurrection of Jesus Christ.[1]

O splendor of God's glory bright
O Thou that bringest Light from Light . . . !

---

1. Cf. *The Christian Story*, rev. ed. (Grand Rapids: Wm. B. Eerdmans, 1984), pp. 97-154; *The Christian Story*, vol. 2: *Authority: Scripture in the Church for the World* (Grand Rapids: Wm. B. Eerdmans, 1987), pp. 254-340.

QUESTIONS TO CONSIDER

1. Think about some of your favorite Christmas hymns. What is the teaching about the Person of Christ found in them? (For example, examine the words of "Hark! the Herald Angels Sing," "O Come, O Come, Emmanuel," "O Little Town of Bethlehem," and "O Come, All Ye Faithful.")

2. From time to time, movies or TV films feature Jesus. What is the idea of the Person of Christ that comes through?

3. Is there a place for Mary in your view of the Christian faith?

4. If a street survey were taken in your town and people were asked what they think about Jesus, what model of the Atonement would appear most often in the responses? Why?

5. If you had two minutes to tell a visitor from outer space what you believe about Christ, what would you say?

6. What are some of the strengths and weaknesses of the various models of the Work of Christ?

7. What do you believe about the resurrection of Christ?

8. In a time of "pluralism," can Christians still believe that Christ is the way that God changed the world? What is our source of authority for giving the answer we do? (The Afterword takes up issues of authority, too.)

V

The Church

Church! We know what that means: First Church, Main Street . . . St. John's by-the-gas-station . . . St. Theresa's by-the-cornfield. Yet preachers and teachers never tire of telling us that church is more than a building. What is that *More?*

We follow the Story to find out. On the heels of Easter, a new chapter begins. In the Bible it's called "Acts." After the actions of Jesus come those of the apostles. Luke, who wrote the book of Acts as well as the one named after him, makes a strong connection between Christ and the church. What is it?

Light permeates his account of how the Christian community came to be. If Easter is a dawnburst, then the first chapter of Acts is the sun rising toward its noonday height. So the author tells of the ascension of the Son/Sun:

> He was lifted up, and a cloud took him out of their sight. (Acts 1:9)

And the creeds of the church herald the ascended Christ, who "sits at the right hand of the Father."

Martin Luther long ago pointed out that the metaphorical eye of faith needs such symbols to express the mysteries of the Gospel. So Luke used the ancient worldview of heaven (as being so many miles away from earth) to declare that the resurrected Christ rose to rule the world. And the eternal bonding of the Father and the Son is portrayed in the imagery of royal chairs and chambers. The true *point* of all this can get lost in disputes on changing views of the cosmos (as now, with astronauts in ascent and the heavens filled with gallactic space).

The Acts account stands true today as it did in the first century. It is telling a *theological* truth — the who and what, the why and wherefore: Jesus Christ is risen to reign over all our world and over the powers and principalities that claim to be in charge of it. In the simple words of the spiritual, "He's got the whole world in his hands!" The royal office of Christ is confirmed!

It may be hard to see this in a world clouded by sin. In fact, Luke's imagery — "a cloud took him out of their sight" — suggests precisely that. But the message is clear: It's really so. Get about your business:

Why do you stand looking up toward heaven? (Acts 1:10)

Soon enough the Light will show its Power:

You will be baptized with the Holy Spirit not many days from now. (Acts 1:5)

And they did go about their business — the nitty-gritty work of feeding and caring for the community, replacing one of its members (Judas), and getting on with the mission.

FIRE AND LIGHT

The forecast of Light and Power to come soon proved true:

> And suddenly from heaven there came a sound like the rush
> of a violent wind, and it filled the entire house where they were
> sitting. Divided tongues, as of fire, appeared among them, and
> a tongue rested on each of them. (Acts 2:2-3)

Flames of the promised Holy Spirit descended from the ascended Sun of God. The clouds parted and the eyes of faith
saw the Light.

Telling

What do these fireworks mean? Some Christians say, "Ah,
tongues of fire. That means the early Christians spoke in
strange tongues like the 'charismatics' do." (It's called glossolalia, mixed speech — sounds that are unintelligible to
everyone but the initiated.) Certainly such "tongues" were
spoken in the early church, as described in other parts of the
New Testament. Glossolalia is also a feature of many other
religions in times of fervor. But something else is going on
here. Onlookers from all over — Rome, Greece, Egypt, Libya
— declare,

> In our own languages we hear them speaking about God's
> deeds of power. (Acts 2:11)

They're telling the Story. The Spirit descends to fire them up
to tell the Story to all the nations!

In the very first sermon in the history of the church, Peter
does just that. He preaches the Gospel in his own tongue . . .

according to the salvation history of his own people, Israel. He speaks of the vision, "the definite plan" (Acts 2:23) that God had from the very beginning to bring the divine purpose to be; he speaks of its trials and tribulations, then of God's Hope, the coming of Jesus Christ — suffering and death, but finally victory! And now *you* too can have it. Come over here where there is Light and Fire — and the people did:

> That day about three thousand persons were added. (Acts 2:41)

The Greek word for this Spirit-sign is *kerygma,* the proclamation of the Good News. God gives the church the tongue to tell the Story. Where the Spirit gathers two or three in Christ's name, there the gift is given to fling the faith joyfully in the air. The church *is* where the Story is told.

Doing

But there is more:

> All who believed were together and had all things in common; they would sell their possessions and goods and distribute the proceeds to all, as any had need. (Acts 2:44-45)

Awesome. The fiery tongues gave these first Christians power to do the undoable.

Give away *all* they have? Pool their possessions for sale, then parcel out the proceeds "as any had need"? To be faithful to New Testament "doing," must we be exactly like the church of the first century? That would eliminate most of us. Here again we face the question of how to interpret the Bible. If we were "inerrantists," we might feel the need to follow this pattern literally. (See the Afterword.) Actually, most of those folks fudge a little here, because they don't follow the "communitarian" practice of the early Christians. They say that what's important is the point of the passage. Right! But we must be consistent and apply this principle elsewhere too.

Well, what *is* the point? For an answer, we have to go back to our beginnings in eternity itself. The Story started in the inner being of God, the triune Life Together. If God is total sharing and caring, is it any wonder that one of the gifts of the Spirit is the same? On earth this means a sharing of things earthly, as surely as in heaven it means a sharing of things heavenly. The church, Christ's own Body on earth, at its very beginning models what the divine sharing and caring is and wills.

Always and everywhere the church is called to live out the love that cares for the basic needs of human beings. The Bible calls this doing *diakonia* . . . "deaconing" — serving. *How* it is carried out depends on the circumstances. The story of early Christians pooling their money and possessions is a showcase of this intention in a period when the apostles expected the end of the world. In our time and place, with its special conditions and expectations, we serve the brother and sister in Christ and the neighbor in need according to the best economic, political, and social wisdom available.

Being

We do live by bread, but not "by bread alone" (Matt. 4:4). There is a life together in the spirit as well as in the body. Acts says,

> They devoted themselves to the apostles' teaching and fellow-
> ship. (Acts 2:42)

"Fellowship" — *koinonia* — is a *being* together as well as a
doing together. It's a tender co-existence that mirrors God's
own triune Life Together. So the Spirit breathes yet another
sign of life into the Body of Christ on earth.

Fellowship was once much more radical than the word
today suggests. It reached out to all the "rejects" of the ancient world. Slaves, women, the poor, the sick, the weak, old
people, infants, widows, orphans — all were drawn in and
dignified. In a world that treated them as nobodies, they
became somebodies, given back their names and their faces.
So much so that the word went around: "See how those
Christians love one another!"

Once again the staggering standards of early Christianity confront us, putting us to shame when we consider how
we are in our churches today. But the heartening message of
koinonia is this: God *does* accept rejects. The grace of God and
the arms of the Body of Christ are big enough to embrace
even the likes of us. *Koinonia* is a *fore-giving* as well as a giving
community, accepting the unacceptable, *sinners* as well as
sufferers.

Koinonia also has a message for a splintered Christianity
— a church divided into competing denominations. Brought
into being by the God who *is koinonia* — the Life Together of
the Persons — the church is by nature one. Therefore it is
called to *be* what it *is:*

> The glory which thou hast given me I have given to them, that
> they may be one even as we are one. (John 17:22, RSV)

Celebrating

The fireworks of God on the birthday of the church seemed to be going every which way. *Telling, doing, being. . . .* Then came yet another burst of the Spirit:

> Day by day, as they spent much time together in the temple, they broke bread at home and ate their food with glad and generous hearts, praising God. (Acts 2:46-47)

Now the direction is . . . God-ward. A grace is given that turns the people to the *Giver*. It's a time for joyful thanksgiving! The people's prayer and praise are joined to the breaking of bread. The table thanks that the early Christians gave was therefore "eucharistic" (full of gratitude). Thankful for Christ's sacrifice, they made their own "sacrifice of praise to God" (Heb. 13:15). Their table's bread and wine became symbols of Christ's own self-offering, and thus became our "eucharist." So we go first to the highest form of Christian celebration — holy communion. And in the same breath we speak of a second celebrative occasion — baptism. These universal rites of the church are *sacraments*, special ways in which Christ keeps his Body on earth alive, "outward and visible signs of an inward and spiritual grace." We might say that they represent the *washing* and *feeding* of the Body of Christ.

Baptism and the Lord's Supper are the two universal sacraments of the church. In Scripture they are instituted by Christ, although scholars debate the authenticity of some of the passages. Such debate notwithstanding, these rites have been enacted by the church from its beginning because they represent the *birth* and *nurture* of the Body of Christ.

Communion

When the apostles broke bread and poured wine in each other's homes, they recalled Christ's broken body and shed blood. But they also believed that something more was happening on these occasions than the remembering of a past event. For them and for us, the symbols *re-present* as well as represent the One who died for us. Jesus Christ himself is host at this Supper! We have communion with the risen Lord. We meet the "real presence" of the glorified Christ. That is why this ordinance has become the "innermost sanctuary of the whole Christian worship."

A full act of Table thanksgiving has the bread of the Word as well as the bread of the oven. The telling of the Story, the proclamation of the Word, is inseparable from its celebration. What a feast this is!

In talking about this feast, the church has sought to walk a fine line between turning it into a magical rite and treating it as merely its own experience of remembering. Again . . . Docetism and Ebionism! And the various names given to the feast reflect the aspects of it that have been most meaningful to one or another part of the church: "holy communion," "eucharist," "the divine liturgy," "the Lord's Supper," "the sacrifice of the Mass."

Ecumenical theology has tried to learn from each tradition, and accordingly sees this sacrament as *thanksgiving to God, communion with Christ,* and *empowerment by the Spirit* for life together and service to the world.[1] And so it is:

1. This sacrament is a "sacrifice of praise and thanksgiving." Here we offer up to God our gratitude for everything

1. World Council of Churches, Faith and Order Paper No. 111, *Baptism, Eucharist, and Ministry* (Geneva: World Council of Churches, 1982).

God is and does. The word for that, "eucharist," is used more and more to describe holy communion. Reflecting this purpose of praise, the "eucharistic prayer" in the standard service is a joyful thanksgiving for all the deeds of God that make up the Christian Story, most of all the sacrifice of Christ on the cross for the sins of the world.

2. As Christians we believe that we meet Jesus at many times in our experience, often as the hidden Christ who comes to us in the world's needs. But "communion" is different. In the world, Christ meets us as we feed the hungry. At the Lord's table, Christ feeds *us*. With the "bread of heaven," as John calls it. But this bread is not an "it," because Christ says, "I am the bread." So we meet yet another mystery of faith.

3. How can all this be except by an inexplicable Power? The triune God is again at work here — the Spirit of the Son of the Father. So the one who presides at the table for the service always invokes the Spirit's presence. By this Power the Spirit makes those who gather around the table a special sign of the Life Together that God wills for all, and sends them away from the table to witness to that Shalom in the world.

While holy communion is sometimes called "the divine liturgy," the word "liturgy" is also used for the way in which public worship in general is conducted. It means "the work of the people," stressing the participation of all of the people of God. So we speak here of "celebrating" as a mark of the worshipping church — both in the eucharist and beyond — using the Greek word *leitourgia*.

Baptism

The first Body was not only fed at the Table. It was also washed in the waters:

Those who welcomed his message were baptized. (Acts 2:41)

To commune with Christ requires entrance into the household of God. Baptism is its doorway.

What happens in baptism? Three things have come to the fore in the church's thinking: (1) we become members of the Body of Christ, (2) we are offered the benefits of Christ's saving Work, and (3) we are called to be ministers of Christ. Baptism, then, has to do with *initiation, salvation,* and *ordination!* Where it is treated with the honor that Scripture gives it on all these counts, there the church is different (John 3:5; Acts 22:16; Rom. 6:3-4; 1 Cor. 6:11; Eph. 5:26; Col. 2:12; Titus 3:5).

When do these things happen? Arguments abound. But the partisans have been talking to each other in recent years and appreciating each other's points of view. Advocates of "household baptism" — those who baptize infants with parents, sponsors, and congregation, making baptism a vicarious act of faith — acknowledge that there is some evidence in the New Testament for household baptism, but not much (Acts 16:15, 31; Acts 18:8; 1 Cor. 1:16), and that a personal decision of faith is basic to salvation (Rom. 5:1; Heb. 10:38). Defenders of "believer's baptism" recognize that Christ *does* welcome children (Mark 10:14) and that one person's faith *can* stand in for another (Matt. 17:14-21). The result has been that the former put a lot more emphasis on personal decision when the child comes of age (in *confirmation* or some other rite) and prepare parents and sponsors carefully for the baptism of a child. And the latter increasingly practice infant *dedication,* understanding it as participation in the family of God with all the privileges and responsibilities that go with such participation. Can this ecumenical approach prevail as we think of baptism as a pilgrimage with various stages? Time will tell.

The book of Acts includes other prayer and praise along with baptism and eucharist. So songs and hymns, private prayers and meditations, and other ceremonies of the church are part of celebrating too. We shall turn to the piety of the people again in our chapter on salvation.

*   *   *

With all the exciting things that happened at the birth of the church, we could get starry-eyed about its condition. Yes, it is something very special . . . the very Body of Christ on earth. But it is a body of *ordinary people* too. Members of the early church had to raise money to survive, just like anybody else. And we still do! They got cranky and argued with each other (1 Cor. 3:1-4). And we still do! The church is a body broken, a community of sinners that is faltering, fragile, and fallen. We can't glamorize it. But the One who lives in its midst, the Holy Spirit, gives us hope for its life and work. And we pray, "Take not thy Holy Spirit from us!"

Models of the Church

Avery Dulles has observed that churches (even denominations) tend to organize their life around one or another theme. He sorts them out into five "models of the church."[2] Four of the five bear a striking resemblance to the signs of the Spirit in Acts 2! The "herald" model, which stresses preaching and teaching, corresponds to *kerygma*; the "servant" model, which stresses deeds of mercy and justice, fits *diakonia*; the "mystical communion/community" model accents *koinonia*; and the

2. Dulles, *Models of the Church* (Garden City, N.Y.: Doubleday, 1974).

"sacrament" model embodies *leitourgia*. Dulles adds the "institution" model, which may be an apple among the oranges, since the other four are all subject to the process of institutionalization — at its best and its worst.

It certainly is true that we tend to tilt toward one or another aspect of the church. That's good if it means using the gift the Spirit gives us. It's not so good if we ignore the other gifts! The early church relished and used every blessing God poured out on it. As such, the early church is the real model for what a congregation as well as the larger church should look like. We pray for the Spirit to enlarge our vision and empower us with the fullness of God's graces.

THE BODY MOVES: MISSION

A living Body fulfills its purpose when it is up and about. The Body of Christ is born to walk and work in the world. This Body in action is the church in *mission*. (The word comes from the Latin *missio*, meaning "to send.") Thus the Spirit turns the Body toward the world "out there"; mission is *outreach*. "The church exists by mission as fire does by burning," says theologian Emil Brunner. While this perspective may stress action too exclusively, it makes a good point. The health of the Body requires motion as well as repose.

Repose and motion, nurture and mission, "inreach" and outreach. Acts 1 and 2 can be read as the *nurture* of the Body of Christ, made alive by the four gifts of the Spirit. Acts 3 and 4 can be seen as the charter of its *mission*. Let's follow what they have to say. We'll be hearing about some familiar themes, but in a new setting and in a somewhat different order.

Doing

> One day Peter and John were going up to the temple at the
> hour of prayer, at three o'clock in the afternoon. And a man
> lame from birth was being carried in. People would lay him
> daily at the gate of the temple called the Beautiful Gate so that
> he could ask for alms from those entering the temple. When
> he saw Peter and John about to go into the temple, he asked
> them for alms. Peter looked intently at him, as did John, and
> said, "Look at us." And he fixed his attention on them, expect-
> ing to receive something from them. But Peter said, "I have no
> silver or gold, but what I have I give you; in the name of Jesus
> Christ of Nazareth, stand up and walk." (Acts 3:1-7)

A miracle of mission! Mission is doing the undoable. And,
as the story of the Good Samaritan illustrates, it is seeing the
unseen. In both cases mission is a deed done *outside* the gate,
on the road. And in each case the power of God mends a
broken body.

The apostolic miracle included a mysterious surge of
healing power. But we would miss the main point if we
reduced the story to the "miraculous" in that sense. Again
the *what* of the matter is the heart of the event, not the *how*.
The Power of God, the Holy Spirit, was given to the Body
of Christ to move outside the gate and serve people by
meeting their bodily needs. The church that continues
Peter's mission will also be empowered to do the deed of
mercy to broken bodies outside their own gates: that church
will see the invisible — the homeless, the hurt, the sick, the
hungry, the maltreated, the war-weary — and serve them.
And when necessary it will challenge the "powers and
principalities" along the way (Acts 5:29).

Telling

> You Israelites, why do you wonder at this, or why do you stare
> at us, as though by our own power or piety we made him
> walk? The God of Abraham, the God of Isaac, and the God of
> Jacob, the God of our ancestors has glorified his servant Jesus.
> (Acts 3:12-13)

Peter begins to tell the Story. Right then and there in the
midst of the deed of mercy comes the Word of the Gospel,
the *Evangel*. Evangelism is getting the Word out to those who
haven't heard it. But true New Testament evangelism is different from much evangelism as it is popularly practiced. In
the early church it was a Word in the midst of a *deed*, word-
in-deed mission. This book in which it is recorded is not the
"talks" but the *Acts* of the apostles. Telling is inseparable
from doing, outside the gate as well as inside it. As one
missionary put it, the acts of mercy and justice are the bells
that call people to church.

Being

The accent in Acts 3 and 4 is on telling and doing. Yet in the
middle of these mission chapters is another note:

> Now the whole group of those who believed were of one heart
> and soul. (Acts 4:32)

Being together is a vital part of outreach. "How those Christians love one another!" was a comment made by citizens of
the first century.

Life in community surely had its power then: the
churches found a place for the sick, the slaves, the orphans,

and the widows. That reaching out continues. Today mission means a welcome to all those who are forlorn, oppressed, and forgotten. Outreach entails a rehumanizing love that makes a place for the last and the least.

Celebrating

> When they had prayed, the place in which they were gathered was shaken; and they were all filled with the Holy Spirit and spoke the word of God with boldness. (Acts 4:31)

If the building "rocked" (NEB), the sight of this joyful company was for outsiders as well as insiders to see! Worship is mission too.

Liturgical mission means letting the world see our celebrating. The gifts of music, art, and literature — the beauty of holiness — together with the joys and solemnities of Christian worship are testimony to the Story. Mission is sending these sounds and sights beyond our walls.

The illustration on the facing page is a visualization of the wholeness of the church and the richness of its people and their gifts—in nurture and mission.

MISSION: OUTCOME

The consequences of doing-telling-being-celebrating mission are wonderful to behold:

1. The personal call issued by the evangelists — "Repent therefore, and turn to God so that your sins may be wiped out" (Acts 3:19) — was answered, for "many of those who heard the word believed" (Acts 4:4). The result of mission is *conversion*. When this happens, an about-face *(metanoia)* takes

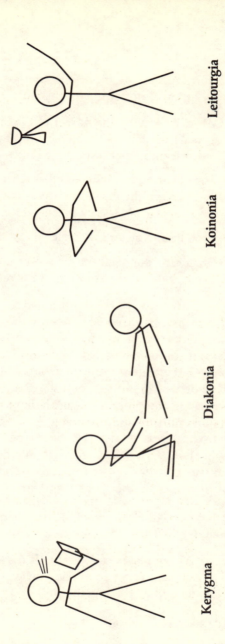

place. Such a turning has these *turning points* — all made possible only by a Power not our own, the Holy Spirit:

Repent — Wrench loose by the power of the Spirit from old idols — whether they be of the flesh or of the spirit. Repentance is turning *away* from the Night.

Believe — Turn *toward* the Light. Confess Christ as your new Lord, trusting in the grace that saves from sin.

Be baptized — Enter the family of Christ, seeing *in* the Light the brother and sister in Christ.

Serve — Minister to the neighbor in need that you also now see in the Light, with "fruits meet for repentance" (Acts 23:20, KJV).

Repent, believe, be baptized, serve — these are the turning points that put us on a new Way. The agony of this new state is the temptation to get stalled at one or another stop. Partial turns mean there are those who get only as far as the trauma of their new birth, fixing upon the "conversion experience" ("repent"), and those for whom believing the right truths is the sum and substance ("believe"), and those who think "going to church" is what it's all about ("be baptized"), and those who hold that doing good is all that matters ("serve"). But true conversion is a full about-face.

2. *Church growth* is another fruit of mission:

Many of those who heard the word believed; and they numbered about five thousand. (Acts 4:4)

Amazing grace. As the New Testament tells us, "God gave the growth" (1 Cor. 3:6). Those in mission believe the promises of God and anticipate the ingathering.

"Small is beautiful," say some Christians; the faithful church will be only the "remnant." Yes, there *is* a time to suffer and be on the outside. That's the next point in the Story. But it's right alongside this one. Because grace is *power* as well as *favor*, we have a right to hope for a *growing* Body! The parable of the sower is a good guide:

> Other seeds fell on good soil and brought forth grain, some a hundredfold, some sixty, some thirty. Let anyone with ears listen! (Matt. 13:8-9)

3. *Confrontation* is as inevitable as conversion in faithful mission:

> While Peter and John were speaking to the people, the priests, the captain of the temple, and the Sadducees came to them, much annoyed because they were teaching the people and proclaiming that in Jesus there is the resurrection of the dead. So they arrested them and put them in custody until the next day. (Acts 4:1-3)

Big trouble! The power structure is put off by the Word. And the deed threatens it as well, as Peter indicates at the trial:

> Rulers of the people and elders, if we are questioned today because of a good deed done to someone who was sick. . . . (Acts 4:8-9)

The Word mated to the act evokes the anger of the establishment. We can't escape the fact that faithful mission makes enemies. If we are asked by Christ to love our enemies, we first have to make some!

In this confrontation the enemies of mission are principalities and powers that believe they are in charge of the future. Here is a military-political-ecclesiastical complex that is threatened by the Word and evidence that Christ is the real Lord. It's a new Day with the Power that goes with the Light. When this message is proclaimed, look out for the opposition. And to it there can be only one response:

> We must obey God rather than any human authority. (Acts 5:29)

Getting It All Together

What would a church today look like if it mirrored the New Testament community described in Acts 2–4? If we made a chart by which to measure ourselves — in nurture and mission, in "inreach" and outreach — it might look something like this:

Nurture (Inreach)	Gifts of the Spirit *and* Marks of the Church	Mission (Outreach)
Preaching and teaching	*Kerygma* (Telling)	Evangelism
Servanthood within (Care for brothers and sisters)	*Diakonia* (Doing)	Servanthood without (Social service and social action)
Life together within	*Koinonia* (Being)	Life together without
Worship	*Leitourgia* (Celebrating)	Festival

THE CARE OF THE BODY: MINISTRY

The Body born, living and moving, needs constant care. Those who so minister to it keep it alive and alert. These caretakers of the Body of Christ are the *ministers* of the church.

Who carries out this *ministry?* All those commissioned to do so. We have already spoken about the first rite of commissioning, *baptism.* Therefore, *all* the members of the Body are claimed for ministry in its waters. The basic ministry of the church is carried out by the "whole people of God." The ministry of Christ continues in the ministry of the Body of Christ on earth:

> Now you are the body of Christ and individually members of it. (1 Cor. 12:27)

While Christ's work among us is not limited to the church, the poet had a point in the saying that "Christ has no hands on earth but yours."

Identity: The Pastoral Office

But what about the clergy? Don't we call them "*the* ministers"? If we confine the word "minister" to them, we've forgotten something *basic:*

> The gifts he gave were that some would be apostles, some prophets, some evangelists, some pastors and teachers, to equip the saints for the *work of ministry,* for building up the body of Christ. (Eph. 4:11-12, italics added)

According to Scripture, the "pastors and teachers" equip the saints — the whole people of God — for *their* ministry. The clergy are the Body-builders, according to Ephesians. Let's look at this more closely.

As Paul teaches in his letter to the Corinthians, the Body of Christ is made up of many members. These different parts do different things. Early in the history of the church the Christian community concluded that God wanted some people to keep reminding it *whose* it is . . . the Body of *Christ*. This constant recollection of its identity — *who* it is — saves the church from amnesia. These caretakers of the Body are custodians of the *memories* of the Body of Christ. Paul calls them "stewards of God's mysteries" (1 Cor. 4:1). In this custodial work, they "equip" the Body for its walk and work.

What are these mysteries and memories? They have to do with the awesome worship of God. Christians gather regularly for telling and celebrating the Story, for "Word and sacrament." In worship we are reminded of whose we are and who we are. But more than that, we actually meet the One to whom we belong! Sunday worship is a weekly celebration of Easter. Christians believe Christ's promise that he will come "where two or three are gathered in my name" (Matt. 18:20) — at this regular time and on other occasions as well.

The people "set apart" (not "set above"!) for taking responsibility for the mysteries and memories are those we have come to call "clergy." They come in all sizes and shapes. Many are local pastors responsible for equipping the saints at First Baptist and St. Agnes — the basic community where the Story is told and celebrated. Some are pastors *of* pastors, since the equippers need themselves to be equipped. These pastors of pastors are described by the New Testament word "bishop" as well as other words like "conference minister" and "superintendent." (Some parts of the church hold that the office of bishop assures the continuity of the church from its apostolic origins onward.) Others equip the saints in other ways: as chaplains, as counselors, as administrators, as teachers. In all cases, in one way or another, those *ordained* by the church — and carefully trained and approved by it — tell and celebrate the Story so that the Body of Christ may be what it is.

Of course, the *whole* people of God tell and celebrate the faith as well! Some may be commissioned to do it in the setting of the church school or as evangelists in the wider world. And all the members of the church take part in worship, and all are called to share the Gospel with friends and neighbors. But some folk — about one percent of the community — are charged with seeing that all this gets done: they are the stewards of the mysteries, the custodians of the memories.

Vitality: The People's Office

And the same thing goes for other aspects of the church's life and witness. We need people to be responsible for the *vitality* of the Body, just as we need some to be responsible for its identity:

> Now there are varieties of gifts, but the same Spirit; and there are varieties of services, but the same Lord; and there are varieties of activities, but it is the same God who activates all of them in everyone. To each is given the manifestation of the Spirit for the common good. (1 Cor. 12:4-7)

It takes many parts to make up a body . . . and the Body. Paul lists in various places the parts that were prominent in the early church: wisdom, knowledge, faith, healing, miracle-working, prophecy, Spirit discernment, tongues, the inter-pretation of tongues (1 Cor. 12); prophecy, service, teaching, exhortation, contributing, aiding, mercy (Rom. 12); apostles, prophets, evangelists, pastors, teachers, saints (Eph. 4).

We have already referred to the distinctions made in Ephesians to describe the relation of pastors and teachers to the rest of the church. In Romans and 1 Corinthians we get a fuller picture of the varied ministry of these "saints." Through their ministry the Body pulses with life! Its vital-ity includes "faith," "wisdom," "healing," "contributing," "helping," "mercy," "tongues" . . . These gifts made things happen.

The energies that keep the Body moving are the *minis-tries of vitality.* Those in the church who exercise these limbs are the caretakers of the Body's life in motion. Through them the Body moves out . . . into the world. This special world-oriented ministry belongs to those in the church whom God has put in the world of daily work and play, eating and drinking, living and dying. We call them "the laity." We take the meaning *not* from the way the world uses the word but from the original Greek meaning of *laos* — "the people of God." The Body was made for life in this world of dailiness. The laity are the "church scattered" across this *secular* terrain. They are the people of God on the front line of mission.

As custodians of the Body's vitality, the powers of move-ment — "doing" and "being" (*diakonia* and *koinonia*) — are their special province. The laity are uniquely positioned (in their place of work, for example) to do and be signs of Shalom. That's why there is a long tradition in the church of thinking about our work as a "vocation," a calling from God to serve the purpose of "life together" in love and justice. Think what the world would be like if every baptized person saw his or her job as a commissioning to a ministry! Or if the church decided that the ministers of vitality should be prepared for their calling . . . and even commissioned to it . . . just as the ministers of identity are! We have a long way to go in honoring the ministry of the church scattered as well as pastoral ministry in the church gathered.

A recent sign that we're making some progress is the recognition that the whole people of God today carry on the very ministry of Christ. The prophetic, priestly, and royal offices of Christ (Chapter IV) are now seen to continue in the *whole* Body of Christ on earth, not just in its clergy. Over the centuries a lot has been said about the clergy's prophetic (preaching), priestly (worship), and royal (leadership) roles. Now it's time to think hard about what these things mean for the ministry of the laity in the world. Challenging times!

Our dividing the functions of the Body into the maintenance of identity and the maintenance of vitality is, of course, not as simple as it sounds. The Body is a living organism with much more mutuality and interconnection. Those ordained to tell and celebrate must also do and be. The doers and be-ers are charged as well to be tellers and pray-ers. And just as the human body adapts when there is some organ failure, so does the Body of Christ: when one or another part weakens, another part falteringly replaces it. Laity spearheading Bible study? Clergy marching for justice? Yes, when needed. Furthermore, "equipping" is a two-way street. Just as pastors and teachers equip the saints, so the saints use their special gifts to equip the pastors and teachers in their own way. Scripture comments on this reciprocity:

> The eye cannot say to the hand, "I have no need of you," nor again the head to the feet, "I have no need of you." (1 Cor. 12:21)

Ministry is mutual.

If we were to try to portray the Body of Christ in a simple stick figure that showed the arms (clergy) and the legs (laity) as the partner ministries, it might look something like this:

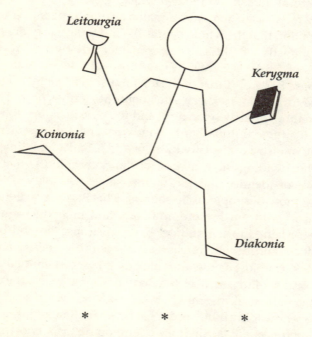

Leitourgia

Kerygma

Koinonia

Diakonia

*　　　　*　　　　*

Church! A gift of God. For all its human failings, the Body is alive and moving, walking and working in the world — by the remarkable power of the Holy Spirit. Like all Christian beliefs, the church is a chapter in a Story that keeps moving on. That's why the Body of Christ is sometimes called the *pilgrim* people of God. It strides ahead with its eyes on "the prize" (1 Cor. 9:24).[3] And the prize is . . . Salvation.

QUESTIONS TO CONSIDER

1. Think about the church or churches you know. Do they specialize in one or another of the signs of the Spirit? Or fit one or another model of the church? What can we learn from other churches?

2. Are you drawn to one or another aspect of the church's life in the Spirit? Are there things you need to learn from other parts of the church?

3. What happens in baptism?

4. What happens in holy communion/the eucharist?

5. What is the mission of the church?

6. Can evangelism and social action be combined?

7. Do the laity have a ministry? If so, what and where is it?

8. What is a pastor? What is the relation of the "clergy" to the "laity"?

3. Cf. *The Christian Story*, rev. ed. (Grand Rapids: Wm. B. Eerdmans, 1984), pp. 155-94.

VI

Salvation

What must I do to be saved? What does it *mean* to be "saved"? What are we saved from?

The answers come thick and fast. Save us from . . . Sickness! Sadness! War! Oppression! Poverty! These cries for help come from people of all times and places.

The Bible has a lot to say about the "cares of the world and ills of the flesh." It tells us that Jerusalem was saved from its enemies, that God wipes away tears, that Jesus healed the sick and preached good news to the poor. Salvation is deliverance from *suffering*.

But Scripture adds something else to our list. If you look up "salvation" in a concordance (a volume of key words in the Bible), you'll find that it has *two* meanings: deliverance from suffering and deliverance from *sin*. This should come as no surprise to us, because the Fall (Chapter II) was a turning point in our Story. That means we have to dig deeper to get at the meaning of salvation.

Karl Menninger, a famous psychiatrist, wrote a book a few years ago called *Whatever Became of Sin?* As a Christian, he didn't want us to let the miseries that preoccupy us hide another fundamental human problem — the one that lies *behind* war, injustice, pollution, hunger, and homelessness. The way he put the problem in the title shows that people today ignore the very issue that the Story holds to be basic.

Some interpreters of Christianity conclude from this that we should stop pursuing *our* issue and "get with it" — forget about sin and deal with suffering! Check the books on religion in the shopping-mall bookstore. They are preoccupied with our problems (mostly personal ones) and how to find relief from them. From popular purveyors of a "health-and-wealth gospel" to the gurus of the New Age, there's not much on the shelves about sin!

The harrowing fact of human suffering *does* confront us on every side. A generation that experienced the Holocaust must never forget it. And ever-present in our troubled world is the possibility of nuclear war, the threat of environmental disaster, and the realities of widespread hunger, heartrending poverty, and homelessness. Put all this together with the uphill battle against drugs, the epidemic of sexually transmitted diseases, and the abuse of one or another class, sex, race, age, or condition, and you have more than most people can take. The plea for deliverance from suffering is a *right cry* from the heart.

But earthly well-being cannot be the *only* real thing. In peering behind scenes of suffering, the eye of Christian faith sees its source in the sin that *inflicts* much of the suffering . . . or that ignores it. We've already met that *arrogance* and *apathy*. We need to be delivered from this source of the human problem — Sin — as well as its consequences. We have a *vertical* accountability before *God* as well as a *horizontal* accountability before the world.

We are covering old ground here — not only the second chapter of the Story, where we met "sin," but also the fourth chapter, where Christ overcame it. The Work of Christ *is* salvation from sin . . . and suffering. But the "benefits" of Christ's Work have yet to be "applied," to use the language of the old teachers of faith. Salvation has happened *already*. It stands waiting to be accepted. And even when we do tap its life-giving waters right now, there's more to come in the future. The theologian H. Richard Niebuhr put it aptly. When a street evangelist asked him, "Are you saved?" he answered, "I *was* saved on Calvary. I *am being* saved by faith right now. I *shall be* saved when the Kingdom finally comes."

Salvation is in three tenses — past, present, and future. Future salvation is the subject of the last chapter of the Story. Here we speak of salvation *now*. We call it "soteriology."

The lives and struggles of two persons symbolize the two sides of the "salvation now" we've been talking about — *Martin Luther* and *Martin Luther King, Jr.* Both of these Christians had a tough time with their contemporaries. The first was rejected by the religious establishment, and the second was killed for his convictions. Each had his own flaws and limitations, of course. But that's why salvation is always by God's grace, not our goodness.

SALVATION FROM SIN

Martin Luther had a hope. An ardent monk and a dedicated teacher, he wanted to do his best for God. He was told that praying, fasting, and penance would cleanse his heart. And that studying Scripture and searching for wisdom would enlighten his mind. But the more he worked to prove his worth, the more uneasy he became. Friends and counselors said, "Relax!" Yet he could not get out of his mind the picture of Christ astride a rainbow urging him ever onward and upward: "Get rid of your selfishness, Brother Martin! Obey the law! Get right with God!"

How can we get right with God — get "righteous"? Every time we make a little progress, thought Luther, we get smug. But pride is the *worst* sin, so we're back where we started! What kind of a way to God is this? "How can I find a gracious God?" he cried.

Luther could not find God, but God found him. His much-thumbed Bible spoke its own Word: "The just shall live by *faith*" (Rom. 1:17, KJV). "Justification by faith" . . . *not* by works. Righteousness cannot be gained by the law, by trying to prove to God how good we are. We can't win God's approval by strenuous activity. It's never enough, and it always tempts us to "think more highly" of ourselves than we "ought to think" (Rom. 12:3). We are made right before God, saved from sin, by *grace,* as Paul stressed in powerful passages (e.g., Rom. 3:21-31). God takes the initiative, not us. All we have to do is receive that Mercy gladly . . . in faith!

And what *is* faith? It begins with *belief* in who Christ is and what he has done for us, especially for the forgiveness of sin wrought on the cross. But belief is not enough. "Even the demons believe—and shudder" (James 2:19). Faith means a deep-down *trust* that God loves and forgives us. Faith is that kind of trust of the heart as well as a belief of the mind. And the Holy Spirit brings it to be.

Luther was overwhelmed by this Good News: God accepts the unacceptable! God loves the unlovely! Those pointing fingers of Christ that he saw as he looked up were *really* outstretched hands at the end of open arms, reaching to lift us up. Christ so welcomes us with infinite tenderness. The hard Work done on Calvary is all there, right now, for us. All we have to do is accept it in trust. And so we are declared righteous before God — justified by grace through faith. What a different view of things! It changed the church, re-forming its ranks. So came the Reformation, with its accent on salvation by grace through faith, and "evangelical" Christianity.

Does that mean that this Reformer found out something about Christianity that no one had known before? Absolutely not. Sometimes Christian basics get covered over or lie undiscovered. Today the followers of Luther and the representatives of the Roman Catholic Church that excommunicated him have *agreed* on some basic things about "salvation by Christ alone," received by faith alone, that formerly deeply divided them, and they have challenged earlier misunderstandings of each other. This certainly is a wonder of our ecumenical times — one of the reasons for a primer on *Christian* basics.

Ecumenical conviction does not stop here. Luther's strong emphasis on God's grace as favor toward us, regardless of our state of sin, could obscure a necessary partner conviction. Where God's grace is, something happens *in* us. The Holy Spirit is right there. That means grace is *power* as well as favor. The Power of God *imparts* righteousness as well as *imputes* Christ's righteousness. The "something" that happens has come to be called *sanctification* — becoming holy as well as being declared a sinner who is holy (acceptable) by a gracious God. Sanctification is growing up in the faith into which one has been "born again" — birth and growth being all by God's initiative, *grace*. We are *not* saved by the good works of sanctification but by "faith alone." But a true believer is like a good tree that brings forth good fruit: when there is real faith, there cannot help but be good works, done in gratitude for what Christ has done and with a new will to do what is right and good.

To take the whole church seriously, including the wisdom of its various parts — those who stress "justification" and those who accent "sanctification" — is a big challenge! But it's the only way we're going to get the *full* gospel. Since we are not yet there in this matter of personal salvation, given our divided traditions, we must go *forward* to the basics.

SALVATION FROM SUFFERING

Martin Luther King, Jr., had a dream — a vision of a world in which black and white children would walk hand in hand across the molehills of Mississippi and the red earth of Georgia. So this man of great hope marched with his people toward a promised land of deliverance, as did Moses and the people of Israel long ago. Deliverance — salvation — has *another* side, both then and now.

In Luther we learned of freedom from bondage to the law — salvation from sin. In King we learn of freedom from bondage to slavery — salvation from suffering. The first is deliverance by grace through faith. The second is deliverance by grace through love.

This second side of deliverance is anticipated in the first. True faith is "busy in love," love of the neighbor as well as love of God — love of God *through* love of our neighbor. Justification expresses itself in sanctification, growth in holiness.

The holy living that King urged on a nation had to do with another aspect of the application of the benefits of Christ's saving Work:

I was hungry and you gave me food, I was thirsty and you gave me something to drink, I was a stranger and you welcomed me, I was naked and you gave me clothing, I was sick and you took care of me, I was in prison and you visited me. (Matt. 25:35-36)

Christ is *present* to those and in those who minister to the hungry and hurt. Grace is busy in the loving deliverance from suffering.

King's witness as a symbol of this second side of salvation has to do as well with *the way* redemption from suffering takes place. It goes to the *sources* of hunger, thirst, nakedness, lack of concern for the sick and the prisoner. . . . King saw that the plight of African-Americans was tied up with segregated schools, jobs, housing, voting, and public accommodations, with a poverty handed down from generation to generation, with a warlike world that cut short resources for addressing all these conditions. It's no accident that "Let my people go!" has become a cry of King's marchers . . . and for a long time has been the great spiritual of black churches.

We saw earlier that in the Story God made life liveable by bringing into being the "orders of creation": the family, the state, the economic order — the institutions, associations, and organizations of human life (Chapter I). The Fall took its toll on these "powers and principalities . . . thrones and authorities" (Chapter II). We can see its results in the pain of oppressed peoples. So these *powers* as well as *persons* need deliverance.

Indeed, that release from bondage has already happened!

He disarmed the rulers and authorities and made a public example of them, triumphing over them in it. (Col. 2:15)

The powers that were created for God's Purpose of Shalom belong to Christ and are re-possessed in his Easter victory.

Those who call them to account today serve Christ's redeeming Work. King's encounter with the political and economic powers that held black citizens in captivity is witness to this second side of deliverance. Salvation, therefore, is *social* as well as *personal;* salvation is deliverance from *suffering* as well as *sin,* bringing *justice* as well as *justification.*

In the present discussion about salvation, "liberation theology" has stressed the social sources of oppression and has served to remind the churches of Christ's call to deliverance from political and economic tyranny. On the other hand, "evangelical theology" has stressed personal salvation. How desperately we need both accents! And more and more, advocates of each are saying so. The *full* Gospel is the Good News of redemption from sin *and* suffering, and the salvation of persons *and* powers. We cannot do without either Martin Luther or Martin Luther King.

SALVATION IN CHRIST AND MODERN PLURALISM

Today we have a keen sense of living on a planet with different religions and worldviews. Television, travel, and the coming of new neighbors from other lands and places make us aware that Christianity is only one of many faiths. And the people of other faiths, or of no faith, live good lives. How can we believe passages in the Bible like John 14:6? There Christ says,

> I am the way, and the truth, and the life. No one comes to the Father except through me.

We experience "plural shock" (the child of future shock and

97

culture shock!) when we hear this claim (and hundreds like it in the New Testament) in our pluralistic world.

And not a few of us get "christological heart failure." These individuals feel that John 14:6 is narrow-minded and that we have to give it up. Various solutions are proposed:

1. A "common core" view, which holds that all religions at bottom are about the same thing. We just call different manifestations of it by different names. "Different strokes for different folks."
2. A "jigsaw puzzle" view, which says that religions are different. We need to take the best from each and make a new world religion.
3. A "Mt. Everest" view, which says that all people find salvation in their religions or in their good moral life, but that Jesus is the highest and clearest expression of this universal condition.

And there are other solutions whose proponents want to preserve some of the uniqueness of Christ but not make salvation dependent on knowing him: an "anonymous Christianity" gained by pursuing whatever goodness and truth one knows, a universal salvation accomplished for all in Christ's death and resurrection but known only to some, and so on.

In short, the church is right in the middle of a great debate on grasping and learning from the widespread fact of pluralism, yet not compromising the Christian basics. At this point we will suggest a way to sort these things out.

Christ *is* the Way God made into the world (Incarnation) and how God turned the Tale around (Atonement). That is a non-negotiable Christian tenet. The compromises made by the three views mentioned will not wash. However, as we've seen in the covenant God made with Noah, there is truth that God scatters throughout the creation for all to see — moral and spiritual wisdom that keeps the Story going. It's a "general revelation," a light seen even after the Fall in our broken-but-not-destroyed mirror (the image of God). Coming from the eternal Word that "enlightens everyone" (John 1:9), it is *Christ* who is the source of whatever truth, goodness, beauty, and holiness there is in human experience, religious or otherwise; this is what Christians believe. The *fullness* of that Light, given the Night of our sin, comes in the Word made flesh (John 1:14). Therefore, Christ is the *Truth* as well as the Way.

The big question we face in this chapter of the Story is about "Life," deliverance, salvation. Do only Christians have it? We've seen that there are *two* sides to salvation: salvation from sin and from suffering/evil. Wherever there is a love that cares for the hurt and the helpless, for the true and the good, there is salvation from the powers and principalities that make our lives unliveable. In fact, Christ teaches us that he is present in just those acts (Matt. 25:33-46). Christians cannot deny the deliverance at work in all humans in this way. By grace we are saved from evil through love, are given the *life* so offered.

Would that all human life were filled with this love! Then God would smile on us and it would be well with our souls. But there is a problem:

No one . . . is righteous, not even one. (Rom. 3:10)

That means we can't count on our tattered now-and-then love to meet the divine expectations. We are not justified by our goodness, our works. In the final analysis, our goodness just doesn't stand up. We are saved from *sin* by faith alone

— given by grace alone. Christians believe that faith comes in meeting the Word and saying Yes! to Jesus Christ. Accordingly, they are eager to get that Word out. The *kerygma* about the forgiveness of sin through the Work of Christ is a central part of the nurture and mission of the church, the offer of the Word of eternal Life.

Well, what happens if a person never hears the Word? Or if it gets put through a bad filter? Are they denied eternal Life? We're talking about hosts of people! And that brings us back to plural shock and all the modern answers. But we cannot go the way of so watering down the faith. The hosts *are* graced by the hidden Christ of Matthew 25 and the wonders so wrought. But they are not denied the revealed Christ either. As the great poet Francis Thompson put it, Christ is the Hound of Heaven. He relentlessly seeks us out with his Word. If it is not heard in *this* world, it will be heard in the world to come. The New Testament teaches in 1 Peter 3:19-20 and 4:6 and hints elsewhere (Matt. 8:11, 12:40; Luke 13:28-30; John 5:25-29; Rom. 10:7; Eph. 4:8-9; Rev. 21:25) that Christ goes to the "place of the dead," as it is said in the Apostles' Creed, to invite us to faith. Thus the pursuit of the least and the last through the corridors of eternity, none being denied the Good News. Christ's faithfulness does not relieve us of the call right now to spread the Good News, for we want to share "the pearl of great value" (Matt. 13:46) that we've discovered.

So we struggle in our day of pluralism to honor *both* the universality and the particularity of the One who is the Way, the Truth, and the Life.[1]

1. Cf. *The Christian Story,* rev. ed. (Grand Rapids: Wm. B. Eerdmans, 1984), pp. 195-221; and *The Christian Story*, vol. 2: *Authority: Scripture in the Church for the World* (Grand Rapids: Wm. B. Eerdmans, 1987), pp. 254-340.

HOLINESS

"Salvation" in doctrine relates to Christian life in *personal* practice. Here the reality of our faith is expressed and tested. The faithful life is a holy life. Growth in holiness ("sanctification") is the hope of the believer.

If faith is genuine, holiness comes naturally. Good seed does produce good fruit! But even the best seed needs the right soil and the right amounts of sun and rain. And it must be cultivated. That means personal holiness has its disciplines. Over the years the church has used Scripture to develop helps about the holy life, helps that include *piety* and *morality*. These are the "vertical" and the "horizontal" aspects of Christian life: our relationship to God and our relations with others — the love of God and the love of the neighbor. They correspond roughly to "salvation from sin" and "salvation from suffering."

Piety

The life and nurture of piety ranges far and wide. At its center is the Spirit-given worship of God discussed earlier *(leitourgia)*. Its most intimate point is *prayer*. Prayer is personal communion with God. Whether private or public, individual or communal, silent or spoken, prayer is direct contact with our waiting God.

And God does wait! How inattentive we are! Even the saintly tell us of their own devotional struggles, their dry periods and desert wanderings. This is also true for us ordinary folk, who need all the help we can get. That's why there are disciplines of prayer — learned ways of focusing our attention and keeping it focused.

Although this primer can't be a manual of devotion, it can offer a theology of prayer. Its starting place is a scriptural passage that has served multitudes in forming their spiritual lives: Isaiah 6, which describes Isaiah's experience in the temple. Many have made it the pattern for public worship. We turn to it here as a guide to the personal life of prayer.

Adoration

In the year that King Uzziah died, I saw the Lord sitting on a throne, high and lofty; and the hem of his robe filled the temple. Seraphs were in attendance above him; each had six wings: with two they covered their faces, and with two they covered their feet, and with two they flew. And one called to another and said: "Holy, holy, holy is the Lord of hosts; the whole earth is full of his glory." The pivots on the thresholds shook at the voices of those who called, and the house filled with smoke. (Isa. 6:1-4)

With Isaiah's vision of God, all else fades from view. Since "no one has ever seen God" (John 1:18), Isaiah experienced and conveyed this meeting in the images of an ancient day, complete with royal throne, seraphic creatures flying about, and a smoke-filled temple. As we enter into his vision, we become intensely aware of the divine Presence, of the majesty, glory, and mystery of God.

"Holy, holy, holy is the Lord of hosts!" indicates the mood of this meeting. Prayer begins with adoration. Prayer can't be communion with God unless the One who is God comes to the fore. Our constant preoccupations, distractions, and diversions tend to obscure the reality that the holy God is right there . . . waiting. To Isaiah, whose heart and mind are fixed on God, GOD appears: "I saw the Lord."

Our praying often starts at a different place — with ourselves. Often we say, "Lord, this is what I need today," or
"This is what this or that person needs right now." Of course,
requests in prayer *are* perfectly in order. (The Christian tradition calls them "petition" and "intercession.") But we aren't
supposed to start there. If we do, that says something about
us and about how we see God: we are still centered in ourselves, and God will have to fit in accordingly. Isaiah teaches
us to let *God* be God. Prayer is lifting the mind's eye and
heart up and out to the Holy One. Prayer begins as it does
with the seraphim — with loving God for God's own sake!

If prayer is hard for us, it may be that we haven't yet
found the gate of "adoration." Our wandering about may
reflect something of where we are in our growth in holiness.

But God is gracious! Even in that state, we can begin . . .
this very moment . . . knowing that God will accept us even
in our unworthiness, and hear us in our praying — loving
us even in our sin.

Part of the self-preoccupation that makes praying difficult lies in cutting ourselves off from other people as well as
from God. No one "is an island," as the poet John Donne
said. That is true in piety as well as in morality. We're made
for life together, just as God is the triune Life Together. Sharing a prayer discipline with others — who pray with you
right then and there, or who are following the same
devotional guide — could be just the support needed. So the
saints have told us and shown us.

Adoration, which means fixing our attention totally on
God, might make it sound like praying is escapist (right "up
and out" of this world!). Sadly, that does sometimes happen
when the "pray-ers" seem to have their heads in the clouds
rather than their feet on the ground. This was not the case

with Isaiah, who spent his life in prophetic witness to God's Shalom. This passage clues us in on his moral — even political — bent. It begins this way:

In the year that King Uzziah died. . . . (Isa. 6:1)

Praying occurs right there in the middle of history! The God we meet in the temple is the same God who engaged in our affairs — from creation to consummation — the same God who actually came into this world and lived among us from crib to cross. Our prayer is to the God of history — to the God of our Story.

To bring the Story in at this point is to recognize that Christians read the Isaiah/Uzziah account in a special way. The Isaiah of the Old Testament meant the Uzziah of sixth century B.C./B.C.E. — thus referring to the God of Exodus and Temple. The seraphic song was directed to a holy God who delivered Israel from Egyptian bondage. For Christians, this prayer includes all these elements, with added praise for God's saving act in Jesus Christ and the new age of the Holy Spirit.

The witness of the New Testament and Christian experience comes out in the seraphic song ("Holy, holy, holy"), during the time of adoration beginning Christian worship, or in the seraphic hymn at holy communion. Here the threefold "Holy" means the triune God of Christian belief. Further, the symbols of enthroned deity, high and lifted up — and the six-winged seraphim and the smoke-filled temple — become for Christians the symbols of the high God who stooped low in Jesus. So Christian prayer is offered "in the name of Jesus" and often *to* Jesus Christ, as is the final prayer of Scripture: "Come, Lord Jesus!" (Rev. 22:20).

Penitence

> And I said: "Woe is me! I am lost, for I am a man of unclean lips, and I live among a people of unclean lips; yet my eyes have seen the King, the Lord of hosts!" (Isa. 6:5)

The holy God of Israel is too much for Isaiah to bear. Divine purity puts him to shame. So too in our life of prayer, the contrast comes sharply home. We remember what the human race did to Jesus, and what we daily do to his cause ("Woe is me!").

Confession of sin proceeds from adoration. When our Lord was crucified, we were there. (And still are in our sins of omission and commission against him.) Admitting our own tendencies and temptations is part of authentic communion with God. Prayer means penitence. It is honest soul-searching — baring to God what is already well known to the all-seeing Eye.

Those who need regular acts of penitence most are precisely those who think they need it least — the "righteous." For we remember that Jesus exposed the self-righteous religious leader who prayed,

> God, I thank you that I am not like other people: thieves, rogues, adulterers. . . . (Luke 18:11)

Instead, Jesus commended the publican's prayer:

> God, be merciful to me, a sinner! (Luke 18:13)

Pardon and Thanksgiving

> Then one of the seraphs flew to me, holding a live coal that had been taken from the altar with a pair of tongs. The seraph

touched my mouth with it and said: "Now that this has touched your lips, your guilt has departed and your sin is blotted out." (Isa. 6:6-7)

Isaiah knew God's mercy from the unswerving covenant made with Israel — through all its ups and downs, its stumbling and straying. The people of Israel knew, and know, that God's love persists in spite of who we are, not because of it. Christians learn of this unconditional covenanting love from Jews.

But how does a holy Love show us mercy without overlooking our sin? That we break God's heart is impossible to overlook. The Story tells us that mercy comes by God's own Self-giving in Jesus the Jew. God's tough Love holds sin accountable yet at the same time takes into itself the consequences for our sin. For Christians, the burning coal that cleanses sin is love itself (Rom. 12:20), and God's own pain is the suffering death of Christ on the cross. Thanks be to God for the grace of our Lord Jesus Christ!

Prayer is thanks-giving. The praying journey moves from who God is and what we are to what God has done (from adoration and confession to thanksgiving). As with Isaiah, our primary gratitude is for what God has done to deal with the basic human problem — sin. Isaiah knew about God's actions on sinners' behalf from the deeds God wrought in the midst of God's people and beyond. So too for the Christian believer who gives thanks for the great deeds of God recounted in the faith. They reside in the very heart of Christian thanksgiving — the eucharist, in the words of a "eucharistic prayer" or the "Great Thanksgiving" in a current communion liturgy:

We give thanks to you, O Holy Lord, almighty and everlasting God, for the universe which you have created, for the heavens and the earth, and for every living thing. We thank you that you have formed us in your own image and made us for yourself. We bless you that when we rebelled against you, you did not forsake us, but delivered us from bondage and revealed your righteous will and steadfast love by the law and the prophets.

Above all we thank you for the gift of your Son, the Redeemer of all people, who was born of Mary, lived on earth in obedience to you, died on the cross for our sins, and rose from the dead in victory; who rules over us, Lord above all, prays for us continually and will come again in triumph.

We thank you for your Holy Spirit and for your holy church, for the means of grace and for the promise of eternal life with patriarchs and prophets, apostles and martyrs. With your church on earth and with all the company in heaven, we magnify and praise you, we worship and adore you, O Lord Most Holy!

As this prayer indicates, thanks is given for the liberation of sufferers as well as for the reconciliation of sinners. The same Isaiah who thanked God for forgiveness of sin time and again lifted up his heart to praise God for deliverance from the pain inflicted on his people — from Exodus to the promise of a new Day when Shalom would dwell in the land. Jesus continued this way of prayerful thanksgiving for the healing, by the mercy of God, of all the hurt. And the Lord's Prayer ends with this exultation: "Thine is the kingdom and the power and the glory forever!" God is the *font of every blessing*.

Petition and Intercession

We've gotten this far in our biblical guide to prayer without yet arriving at what many think prayer really is: asking God for something. Actually, Isaiah's only request (yet to come) is that God will send him into action! But there is no doubt that prayer includes petition and intercession. True, petition and intercession do not figure in this "inaugural vision" of Isaiah's

107

ministry. But we can't get an entire theology of prayer from one passage in the Bible. We need David as well as Isaiah.

Accordingly, we turn to the Psalms to learn about the kind of prayer we know so well:

> How long, O Lord? Will you forget me forever? How long will you hide your face from me? How long must I bear pain in my soul, and have sorrow in my heart all day long? How long shall my enemy be exalted over me? (Ps. 13:1-2)

Here's a prayer that's up front about suffering, a complaining prayer, one ready to argue with God about what a raw deal the "pray-er" is getting. That's honesty in prayer. If we can't be honest in prayer, where can we be honest? Tell it like it is to God. Speak about the pain and misery.

Grieving to God is the underside of thanking God — facing the worst as well as the best. Yes, prayer is for arguing with God too! In prayer we can appeal to God for justice that does not seem to be on the way. The psalmist did:

> Hear a just cause, O Lord; attend to my cry; give ear to my prayer from lips free of deceit. From you let my vindication come; let your eyes see the right. (Ps. 17:1-2)

Frankness becomes — that is, adorns — faithfulness. Let prayer be without deceit, without fawning and fakery.

And let it be still more:

> The Lord answers you in the day of trouble! The name of the God of Jacob protect you! May he send you help from the sanctuary, and give you support from Zion. . . . May he grant you your heart's desire, and fulfill all your plans. (Ps. 20:1-2, 4)

Bold words. Bring all your needs to God Almighty, the psalmist tells us. And so does Jesus. The Lord counsels us to offer a prayer with these petitions:

> Give us this day our daily bread. . . . Deliver us from evil.

And by the power of God, Jesus did these things himself, feeding the hungry, healing the sick, liberating the captive, giving friendship to the friendless. As the popular hymn says,

> What a Friend we have in Jesus, all our sins and griefs to bear!

Bring the ills of the flesh and the cares of the world to the throne of grace!

Our requests can be for the highest hopes of life with God, for the cause of the church, for the spread of the mission. But we can also bring to God the needs for food and clothing and shelter. Our requests can be modest and lowly.

When prayers are for others, we call them "intercessions." When they are for ourselves, they are "petitions." And there are no limits except those set by the purpose of God. Prayer toward God is prayer that fits the God it is directed toward. That gives us pause, tells us something about the shaping of our petitions. That's why adoration, confession, and thanksgiving set the stage for petition and intercession. So we pray "give us this day our daily bread" in order that we may be strengthened for our service to the God we adore and serve. We pray "deliver us" from the evil of the cancer cell and the careless driver so that we might be healthy and whole in faith, hope, and love. We intercede in prayer for others — those named by the congregation and the pastor on Sunday morning or on our own list in the dark of night — so that they might better seek and serve their God. We pray for the end of war and for the beginning of justice because that's the way it is in the realm of God.

We make our petitions and intercessions with confidence that God listens to us. However they are answered

— in God's way, not our ways, with a "Yes" or a "No" — we make our requests with the same trust the psalmist taught us:

> The Lord is my shepherd, I shall not want. . . . Even though I walk through the darkest valley, I fear no evil. . . . Surely goodness and mercy shall follow me all the days of my life, and I shall dwell in the house of the Lord my whole life long. (Ps. 23:1, 4, 6)

Hearing the Call

> Then I heard the voice of the Lord saying, "Whom shall I send, and who will go for us?" (Isa. 6:8)

We return to Isaiah. His final moves are universal ones, according to the testimony of Scripture and the saints. He is now on the listening end as this event draws to its climax.

Prayer is listening, too. God speaks to us in our silences. While this Word can be loud and clear, God also can be heard in a "still small voice" (1 Kings 19:12, RSV). Praying is also waiting. The Voice may speak to us in the depths of our being, or come to us via the turbulent surfaces of life, in events and people. The Whisper may come in the more serene settings of natural beauty or divine worship. For Isaiah it came in the temple. For us . . . ?

> Be still, and know that I am God! (Ps. 46:10)

While we cannot be sure where it will be, we can be certain of what it will be: a call. "Whom shall I send?" We've already heard the assurance; now we hear the invitation. Grace abounds! Sin is forgiven; brokenness is healed. Now *be what you are,* favored and empowered for God's purposes.

With the gift goes the responsibility, accepted from the God of tough Love.

Answering the Call

And I said, "Here am I; send me!" (Isa. 6:8)

Praying is committing. In prayer as well as in what comes after it, we pledge our allegiance to our Maker and Redeemer. The other side of covenant is our covenant promise to receive and live in response to God's Promise. For Isaiah it was the beginning of a new life and ministry. For us each time as we rise from prayer it is the "first day" of our new life and ministry.

Take my life, and let it be
Consecrated, Lord, to Thee.
Take my moments and my days;
Let them flow in endless praise.

Morality

With morality, as with piety, we speak of the most elementary things. Libraries have been written about its complexities. Its issues remain matters of heated debate. Even the name is at issue — is it "morality" or "ethics"? Here is one way to think about these things.

Morality has to do with the life of holiness as it touches other people, ourselves, and the world around us. If piety is "vertical," morality is "horizontal."

Christian morality is guided by the vision of Agape-Shalom, our living toward it in the day-to-day realities of our world. From time to time on this journey we are faced with a yawning abyss of evil and uncertainty. So Christian morality must always take into account the *vision,* the daily *realities,* and the occasional *abyss.* That's why we're going to explore morality at three levels: Heaven, Earth, and Hell.

Heaven

The "Kingdom of Heaven" is the last chapter of the Christian Story. We are not there yet, but its light shines back on us in every moment of our decision-making. In this Realm of God, Agape reigns; perfect love prevails. The world lives in its intended togetherness, reflecting what God is and Jesus was. To make a place for Heaven in our morality means to make all our choices in the light of this Goal. Because Heaven is our moral home, we can settle for nothing less than its standards.

Having Heaven on our mind makes Christians radicals. We are restless with anything short of our homeland, "strangers and pilgrims." The world will not be right until swords are beaten into plowshares and spears into pruning hooks, until the wolf and the lamb lie down together, until each person eats from his or her own vine and fig tree. As the spiritual puts it, "Keep your eyes on the prize. Hold on!"

A Kingdom-oriented morality will measure every moral issue by that perfect standard. That means war is wrong because there is no violence in Heaven. (No weapons — not even police clubs — will be found on the streets of the New Jerusalem.) Oppression is unthinkable because there is not a single injustice in the realm of God. Poverty, hunger, and homelessness are unacceptable because there is peace and plenty in the World to Come. Every life is inviolable because God's eye is on every sparrow, and the heavenly Father numbers the hairs of every head — from the fetus in the womb to the comatose patient in the nursing home, from the tiniest sea urchin to the largest mammal, from . . .

Come on! How can all this be? Just take the food chain, you might say. Nature *has to be* "red in tooth and claw," as the poet Tennyson said. We *have* to have police forces. To save a mother's life, a fetal life may have to be ended. . . .

Yes, life on Earth *is* different from life in Heaven. We live on a terrain short of Heaven. We'll get to that in a minute. But even on Earth, we Christian pilgrims keep our eyes on the Prize. We are drawn ahead by the vision of a *new* Earth. We never settle for the dog-eat-dog — or even the cat-eat-mouse — realities all around us. That means we are called to be the world's "critics-in-residence," never letting it settle comfortably into the status quo, always pressing it toward higher approximations of the laws of the New Jerusalem.

For the church to keep in mind its vocation as the conscience of the Kingdom, it needs within its own ranks a company of *visionaries*. It should value these "heavenly absolutists," whoever they are: the peace churches that stand against all violence, the pro-life movement that fights for fetal dignity, the environmental activists who defend the tiniest sparrow. These are blessed irritants who keep us on the way toward the Not Yet.

Treasure them we must, and honor their witness, but Christian morality is *not only* about Heaven. It's about *Earth* and *Hell* as well. Each realm has its claim upon us. And each has its temptations. One overarching temptation is to consider one moral realm to be the *only* one, to make its insights an *ism*, to reduce all decision-making to Heaven, or to Earth, or to Hell. With regard to the Heaven-stormers, that means "beware the utopian" who does not grasp how deeply sin has a hold on the Earth or recognize the agonizing ambiguity of much moral decision-making. *Perfectionism* is the flaw of pure visionaries. Yes, we *need* the vision of Heaven. But it can't be mistaken for the reality of Earth.

The painful encounter between the two can be seen by applying the Good Samaritan story to the Earth we often meet. Consider the Samaritan arriving on the scene *during*, not after, the assault. Perfect love would require him to turn the other cheek to the assailants. In a fallen world where sin exploits vulnerability, there will be two victims instead of one . . . and no one to bind up the wounds and take the hurt to the hostel.

Given the second chapter in our Story — the Fall and its effects on perfect love — the heavenly vision has to connect with earthly realities. So we must travel to that next plane of decision-making.

In doing so we must be wary of the temptation to *eliminate* the heavenly standard. For example, an old "two-kingdom" theory argues that perfect love is fine for church and personal relations but impractical, even harmful, in the real world of politics and society. To set bounds to the sin that wreaks havoc in this worldly kingdom, we need only "law and order." So the Earth has its "ism" too, a *legalism* in which the tender pull of Heaven is no more and the hard choices of Hell disappear. Without losing sight of these partners, let us step toward the Earth.

Earth

We live in this land day in and day out. The Earth is the terrain of job, home, government, leisure, health care, eating and sleeping, living and dying. Deciding what to do and which way to go is a daily must. What light can our faith shed on all this?

114

In this puzzling world, Scripture and Christian tradition help us with their earthly rules. Chief among them for the biblical peoples are the Ten Commandments. Notice that the Commandments are full of "Thou shalt nots" (Exod. 20). The "nots" tell us that there is already something askew in this land. It's *not* Heaven, where love reigns, but Earth, where sin dwells. So we have moral *law*, the second table of the Commandments, with its "Thou shalt nots" about stealing, lying, adultery, killing, and covetousness. Evil does have a foothold on this turf, but the Commandments say, "So far and no further."

"Rules" are never popular. But we're going to have them one way or another — the "rule" of unrighteousness or the rules of righteousness. In the Christian Story, sober as it is about our sinfulness, the old standards of Mt. Sinai still have their place. Jesus honored them and then went on to flood them with the Light of Heaven (Matt. 5–7). All humans have some sense of them through the lesser light of "general revelation" or Noah's covenant. These negatives won't bring Heaven . . . but they can make for a better Earth.

We get from the Commandments something more than rules for personal living. They have implications for society too. The Old Testament works some of these out in its demands for justice for the poor and the oppressed, the hungry and the forgotten. And the New Testament has built upon these demands in the teaching of Jesus and in the practice of the early church. Accordingly, these basic guidelines for earthly action are more sweeping moral laws. Three usually come to the fore: *justice, freedom,* and *order.*

Justice is giving people their due. In a world where one is tempted to take away from another what is not his or hers (stealing and murder), justice says, "No . . . Thou Shalt Not."

Equal justice is justice in its highest form. For Christians, equality on Earth bespeaks the co-equality of the Persons of the Trinity and life together in the Reign of God. Just so Heaven pulls Earth toward it!

Freedom is the moral law that protects a person's right to choose, a right grounded in the image of God given to each and finally in God's own freely chosen Life Together.

Order is the moral law that sets limits on the chaos that can result when people just do what they want. We are not free to be unjust or to take away another's freedom.

A little out ahead of these standard moral laws — closer to Heaven — is the law of *peace*. Not the pure peace of the heavenly Shalom but an approximation of it in a mutual respect for others, which makes life liveable. Without it we could destroy the world; hence its practical earthly character.

Hard decisions come when we have to take these general laws and make them specific. But here we get a little help from our friends. The Christian community and/or the biblical peoples and/or the human community on occasion get themselves together to translate the great earthly principles into the needs of a particular time and place. So emerges a broad consensus on what justice means for certain specific issues. For example, in the 1960s a conviction grew in the churches that justice required securing for black citizens equal rights in voting, housing, education, jobs, and public accommodations. These applications, halfway down the line from general principles, become what some call "middle principles." More recently, justice for disabled people has come to mean equal access to buildings. This conviction has its effect not only on public policy but also on whether or not a church builds a ramp to its front door. In this way our general principles climb down from the sky to where we live.

There are other guidelines of a more long-standing nature that aid us in making moral decisions on Earth. These have to do with the way human life is organized around our basic needs. We have already met these guidelines in the early chapters of the Story: the *orders* of creation . . . and later of preservation.

To sustain human life itself — to free it, order it, and make it just and peaceful — we are bonded together in certain communities. Christian teaching returns time and again to three universal orderings of human life: the family, the state, and the economic order. Let's look at one of these — the family. As we do, we also connect with morality fore and aft — Heaven and Hell.

An Order of Preservation: Marriage and the Family

God "sets the solitary in families." Human beings are made for life together: as in God, so with us. The human family is a special laboratory for God's Purpose. The intimacy of its life, with both its challenges and its possibilities, makes it so.

The human family, according to Scripture, begins in the relationship of a man and a woman. From the beginning of creation, God "made them male and female," intending them to be together:

> For this reason a man shall leave his father and mother and be joined to his wife, and the two shall become one flesh. . . . So they are no longer two, but one flesh. (Matt. 19:5-6)

This union reflects the very image of God in us:

117

> So God created humankind in his image, in the image of God
> he created them; male and female he created them. (Gen. 1:27)

As we've noted in Chapter I, the male-female bond in marriage is intended to reflect something of the Life Together in God. The fact that "knowing" is the biblical word for sexual union is an indication of the importance of this sign and the high esteem in which it is held in Scripture.

The human fascination with sexuality is tied up with its sense of this importance as well as with the obvious physical allurements. And the corruption of sexuality in many and various ways bears its own strange testimony to the same. The Christian commitment to sexuality as fulfilled in conjugal union and the lifelong commitment of a man and a woman is the way the church honors God's gift and the reason why it celebrates it in the marriage service. Indeed, in the service the marriage covenant self-consciously reflects the unconditional Agape. That's the meaning of the pledge of each partner to continue to be faithful to the other through thick and thin — "in sickness and in health, in joy and in sorrow, for better or for worse, till death do us part."

While marriages reflect the very love of Heaven (are "made in Heaven," in that sense), they are of the Earth, earthy. *Eros* — love by attraction — as well as unconditional Agape love is part of this bonding of a man and a woman. Erotic love is perfectly natural to an embodied existence. Just as the material world is created good, so sexuality is a gift of God.

But there is an enigma here. The same Jesus who extols the "one flesh" of marriage also says that the inhabitants of Heaven "neither marry nor are given in marriage" (Luke 20:35). And Christ himself did not marry. These qualifications tell us that marriage is an order of *creation* that is necessary for life together under the conditions of earthly existence. But just as there is no longer a church in the World to Come, so there is no longer marriage (and family) when the "spiritual body" dwells in the final Realm of God. One wing of the church has made a special point of this, urging on some the celibate life as a reminder of the World to Come and thus of the earthly nature of conjugal union. While those in such a state can never claim superiority, the single life can be a vocation too.

As noted, one of the purposes of marriage is to bear witness to God's own "unitive" and covenanting love. But there is another purpose in marriage: the bearing of children. Conjugal union is fulfilled in a *family*. Sexuality is a gift given to the human race — and to all creation — in order that it might carry the Story forward. The coming of the next generation depends on the birth and nurture of children. Indeed, procreation is a reflection of God's own will for creation — the one is human love; the other, divine love.

The bearing of new life has sometimes been seen as the sole purpose of marriage. Time and place have had their influence on this single-minded view. (Influential factors have included infant mortality, war, economic factors, and so on.) So too, the absence or presence of means of preventing conception have had their effect. In our time and place, both the technological means for preventing conception during sexual union and the increasing awareness of conjugal companionship as one of the partner purposes in marriage have led most churches to teach that the blessing of children is not the same as limitless conception. *That* procreation is a wise and loving end to marriage is unquestioned. *When* to have children and *how many* children to have depends on the larger framework of love. Indeed, circumstances — such as pregnancy endangering the life of the woman or the intrusion of infertility

— may even affect the *how*. In such circumstances adoption can provide the blessing of children. And technology poses questions of alternative birthing for which the church as yet has no "middle principles."

One of the moral issues that produces the most agitation among Christians as well as in the wider society is associated with the blessing of having children: the state of the unborn. Once a fetus comes to be and a human life is set on its path, is the choice to terminate that fetus moral or immoral? By raising this question, we have moved from the Earth of "middle principles," from guidelines for enriching life to guidelines for inflicting death or preventing it. We need those too. But they have to do with *Hell*, "Hell on Earth." This is our last level of moral decision-making. We move now to this abyss.

Hell

The theologian Reinhold Niebuhr once said in a vivid figure of speech that Hell on Earth is when both horns and all four feet of the devil show themselves. Hell comes upon us when we are traveling along the surface of daily life, confident of our moral map, and suddenly we fall into one of its bottomless pits. In this chasm, all is darkness. We can't see our maps anymore.

In Hell there is *drastic* ambiguity. Anywhere we turn seems to be a move in the wrong direction. Every option before us is a bad one. We are faced only with evil choices. When all our options involve hurting somebody, what are we to do? In Hell we are forced to choose the *lesser* evil. We attempt to discern what that is by the best lights we have, shed by a match lit to read our map, Scripture, and by a few candles in the hands of our friends in the Christian community who also share our descent into the abyss or experience vicariously our plight.

These perplexities come home to us in some of the family issues just discussed. We have spoken of the nobility of marriage, yet this estate can be violated. Marriage can become hell: consider the battered woman, the faithless spouse, the abused child. When these tragedies are involved, can the marital bond be sustained "till death do us part"? Life in these bonds may in fact be "death." By the searchlight of heavenly love and by the earthly standards of justice, freedom, and order, those involved may decide that the continuation of the bonds cannot be tolerated. Because the covenant has been implicitly broken, it may come to the point of choosing to explicitly end it. The choice of divorce (or annulment in some traditions) was not contemplated in the marriage covenant and cannot be considered "good." But in the situations mentioned it may be a lesser evil than the terror rained down on the innocent parties in the family bonds. A Christian makes such a decision in *community* if at all possible. A third party may be able to provide a perspective that those directly involved, who are necessarily partisan, may find hard to achieve. This is the role played by the pastor or marriage counselor or support group. They carry into Hell the heavenly light of life together.

We press even deeper into Hell when we consider not the death of a relationship but the death of a person. In the Heaven of Agape-Shalom, all is life, and death is unthinkable. On Earth, human life made in the divine image is inviolable. The commandment says, "Thou shalt not kill."

In Hell, however, we may be confronted with something more ambiguous than the simple and clear alternative — to be or not to be, to kill or not kill. We may be faced with killers whose onslaught against the race can be stopped only by peril in kind. An earlier generation faced with Hitler's slaughter of six million Jews determined to resist him with the weapons of war. At other times tyranny has been confronted by a militant movement for freedom. Thus the just revolutions of yesterday and today. Such acts — war against tyranny, revolution against oppression — *are* evil. But the alternatives are worse. Christians may have to make agonizing choices.

But Christians do so *differently* than others. We know that these acts stand in contradiction to the Kingdom of Heaven. Accordingly, when engaged in them in the kingdom of Hell, we act in *penitence and faith*. We confess our sin and call upon God's forgiveness. We also assess such acts in community. We seek the counsel of sisters and brothers to ascertain whether a particular action is a "just revolution," to use the language of the tradition. And now there are proposals of "just abortion." In struggling to understand when such evil action might be *fit*, although never *good*, the church asks in pain about the circumstances that might warrant such a heartrending decision. Some speak of "middle principles" needed to make such ambiguous choices, so the community may have a more formal role in shedding light in the dark corners of moral options.

As in the other kinds of moral choice, so too in Hell we find an "ism." The perfectionism of Heaven and the legalism of Earth are here joined with the *situationalism* of Hell. In its extreme form it insists that circumstances so alter cases that rules get in our way. It says that "faith and facts" are all we need to make up our minds. Or it says, "Let love be our only light." With a conscience untroubled by some abstract "good" or "right," let us decide what is the loving thing in each new situation.

Missing here is the wisdom of Heaven that holds us as decision-makers accountable to the absolute law of love in behavior as well as attitude. Missing too is the community we need in the Hell that has no illusions about capacity and desire to do the loving thing. Missing as well is the wisdom of the biblical peoples about the codes and moral laws that make and keep life human. Yes, there *are* exceptions to our rules. But situationalism makes the exception *into* the rule.

There is no way to escape the Hell on Earth into which we stumble from time to time. We prepare for it even as we undertake much of our moral decision-making on the solid Earth, equipped with the light that Scripture and tradition give us to walk there. And our walk is always toward the heavenly Realm of God.

There is no salvation without the grace that brings to be

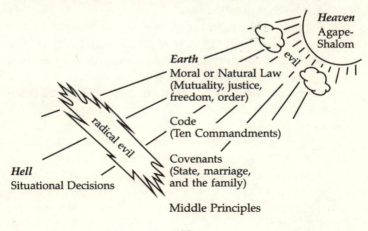

123

a *faith* busy in *love,* expressing itself in the *moral* life according to the ethics of *Heaven, Earth,* and *Hell.* So morality joins piety in the life of *sanctification* that grows from the birth of *justification.*[2]

QUESTIONS TO CONSIDER

1. If someone asked you if you are saved, what would your answer be?

2. Look up in a Bible concordance the references to "salvation." Does it have different meanings? If so, what are they? If not, what is the one meaning?

3. What is "faith"?

4. What is the relation of "justification" to "sanctification"?

5. Is there "social salvation" as well as "personal salvation"? If so, what does it mean?

6. Where do the moral teachings of the Sermon on the Mount (e.g., Matt. 5:38-42) fit into your life and theology?

7. Consider one pressing moral issue and apply the Heaven/Earth/Hell approach to it.

8. What are the different kinds of prayer? Do you practice some or all of them?

2. Cf. *The Christian Story,* pp. 209-14.

VII

Consummation

We don't know what's comin' tomorrow
Maybe it's trouble and sorrow . . .

What *is* coming tomorrow? We all wonder what lies ahead. Today "the future" is much with us. Apocalyptic predictions abound: "The End is near! Armies are on the march! The battle of Armageddon awaits!" Some claim that true believers will be taken into heaven by Christ at "the rapture" to avoid the coming "tribulation." Others warn: "Terrible things are in store — not supernatural but natural catastrophes: atomic holocaust, environmental disaster. . . ."

The age-old teaching of the church has been otherwise. Different from both the religious and the secular fears and frenzies, it has another reading of the Story's last chapter about the End, the *eschaton*. Hence the doctrine called "eschatology."

Christians look forward in *two* ways — long-range and short-term: Last Things and Next to Last Things. Our hope is for both Tomorrow and tomorrow. Last Things, the final Future, have to do with the end of the world . . . the End of the Story. Next to Last Things have to do with the future that lies ahead of us — in both this world and the next — *before* God's grand Finale. That means next month, next year, in the year 2000 and afterward — in *this* world. Next to Last Things also include what the faith holds to be true about life *after* death but *before* the consummation of all things.

Because we are not there yet, the Bible and the church have been reserved about describing the Future/future. Both Scripture and tradition stress *mystery* and use lots of picture language. We see not through a window clearly but "through a glass, darkly" (1 Cor. 13:12, KJV). The glass is *translucent,* not *transparent.* It's like stained glass, giving enough light to see by. Enough to sing about the mysteries from our hymn-books! The windows into the Future inspire the hymns and prayers of worship rather than give us a clear view of the other side.

Four such prominent windows have gotten the attention of Christians through the ages. These visions, mentioned in the ancient creeds of the church, are regularly alluded to in graveside Scripture and prayers: *the resurrection of the dead, the return of Christ, the last judgment,* and *everlasting life.*

LAST THINGS

Window One: The Resurrection of the Dead

Some religions teach that our final destiny is to be in a world of immortal souls detached from our bodies. Others hold that our final hope is in the merging of our individual spirits into the Great All — as drops of water enter the sea. On the other hand, secular views hold that "when you're dead, you're dead." According to them, our best hope of immortality is to live on through the influence we've had on others.

The Christian Story differs from all these opinions. It speaks of "the resurrection of the dead" (1 Cor. 15:42).

What is that? Christians believe that we've *already seen it:*

> Christ has been raised from the dead, the first fruits of those who have died. (1 Cor. 15:20)

In Christ, that is what *we* all shall be!

Christ's resurrection was not confined to his "soul." The skeptical Thomas put his hand in the risen Christ's wounded side. And the Apostles' Creed speaks of "the resurrection of the body." But, according to Paul, this is a very *different* kind of body — a spiritual body; he says,

> Flesh and blood cannot inherit the kingdom of God. (1 Cor. 15:50)

Christ's own Easter body is reported to have passed through physical barriers, so it must have been different. Here we are indeed given a stained-glass view, not a picture-window view!

Notice that if our bodies have eternal significance, then we can't so spiritualize faith that we ignore the condition of bodies — our own or others. Love of our neighbor in need means that we are concerned about the neighbor's bodily needs — health, food, clothing, shelter. At both the beginning and the end of the Christian Story, God loves us as we are — in our *total* condition, bodies included.

The resurrection of the dead has a sober side as well. No one's life ends at death. According to Scripture, *all* will be resurrected (Rom. 14:10). There is no way we will disappear from view and avoid accounting for the life we have lived.

That issue appears in our third window, so we'll defer saying more about this until the "final judgment."

Window Two: The Return of Christ

The Bible paints some vivid pictures of Jesus' return to earth . . . "on the clouds." The biblical authors make a terribly important point with this symbol: while just a few witnessed the risen Christ, one day

> every knee should bend, . . . and every tongue should confess that Jesus Christ is Lord. (Phil. 2:10-11)

That's why Christians hope for a *second* coming of Christ. What he accomplished in God's hidden realm will someday be revealed to all.

How this will happen is another matter. The New Testament uses the language of first-century science to speak about it. At that time people believed that the earth was flat, with heaven "up" so many miles and hell "down" so many miles. In this familiar "three-decker universe," Christ's return would naturally be portrayed as a descent from above right down through the clouds, just as his rising into heaven was pictured as an ascent right up through the clouds (Acts 1). In our day and age, when space probes have been in the heavens, things look different. This is another reminder to us that the Gospel is about the *what*, not the *how*, of the matter.

But some people still insist they know the latter, including the *when* and *where* of it. They are convinced that the End is coming soon and that key events will take place in Israel — in fact, they claim, those events began with the establishment of the state of Israel in 1948. These "apocalyptic" views have always been popular in times of high anxiety. Right now they include various kinds of "pre-millennial" teachings — for example, the view that Christ will come to set up a thousand-year reign of peace after defeating the foes of God in the great battle of Armageddon — with different camps holding opposing views on the schedule of the "rapture" of believers: will it happen before, during, or at the end of the anticipated seven years of tribulation? After that, Satan returns to challenge Christ, only to be decisively defeated, and that event ushers in a new heaven and earth.

Old-line Christianity has never considered these blue-prints of the End to be part of the basics. It has taken Paul's advice:

> Now concerning the times and the seasons, brothers and sis-ters, you do not need to have anything written to you. For you yourselves know very well that the day of the Lord will come like a thief in the night. (1 Thess. 5:1-2)

And it has taken Luke's advice:

> It is not for you to know the times or periods that the Father has set by his own authority. (Acts 1:7)

And Matthew's too:

> About that day and hour no one knows. (Matt. 24:36; cf. Mark 13:32)

However, the dramatic pictures of the End *do* have a theological importance. We have to learn to interpret the occasional mysterious passages in places like Daniel and Revelation in the light of the Bible's overall Story. The "anti-Christ" who is pictured as arriving in the last days is a symbol of how evil persists to the end of time, so we can never be naive about history going ever onward and upward. The belief in a thousand-year reign of peace encourages us to hope for real gains for Shalom in this world, however much each advance is flawed. And the sense of impending doom that marks the apocalyptic is a reminder of how precious the time is that we have left.

To believe *that* Christ "will come again" — the heart of the matter — is to trust that Jesus' prayer will be answered: The Kingdom *is* coming, and God's will *shall* be done on earth as it is in heaven. "There's a great Day comin'!"

Christ comes for *reckoning* as well as for redemption. The Apostles' Creed minces no words: "He shall come again to judge the living and the dead."

Window Three: Final Judgment

When the Son/Sun of God shines in all the world, everything comes to light, exposed to the rays of righteousness:

> For we must all have our lives laid open before the tribunal of Christ, where each must receive what is due to him for his conduct in the body, good or bad. (2 Cor. 5:10, NEB)

This is a fearful moment. What can be more painful than to look with an honest eye at what we have been and done? Is it any wonder that the searing of our conscience by this light has been portrayed in biblical symbols of fire?

Who then is judged? Better to ask who is *not* judged. Are there *any* who can plead their innocence before this judgment bar of perfect love and light? In eternity as well as in time, this is the hard truth:

> There is no one who is righteous, not even one. (Rom. 3:10)

Final judgment can no more stand or fall on the basis of our presumed "good works" than the judgment we face before God in this life. Everything we have is by *grace*, received in *faith*. And there is another thing to consider: Who is the Judge? *Jesus Christ* himself. And because this is so, the whole matter is seen in a new light. Christ is the *savior* of the world, not its condemner:

> God did not send the Son into the world to condemn the world, but in order that the world might be saved through him. (John 3:17)

This Light that exposes our sin on Judgment Day is the radiance of *Agape*, the love of the unlovely and unlovable. In eternity as well as in time, we confront an awesome love that accepts the *unacceptable*.

Major questions immediately pose themselves. Does this mean that *everyone* is saved? What about all the places in the Bible that speak of the sheep and the goats, eternal blessedness for some and eternal damnation for others? What *are* the Christian basics about heaven and hell?

As before, when we come to a frequently debated part of the Story, we look at the conversation about it in the Christian community. At this window there is much dispute. We look at the sharp differences and ask if there is a way beyond them.

Night and Light

The majority view in Christian history has declared a twofold destination for the human race, which is divided into two groups: the saved and the damned, "the sheep [and] the goats" (Matt. 25:32ff.). There are plenty of passages that can be understood in this way (Matt. 10:32-33; 25:31-46; Luke

16:19-31; John 3:36; 5:25-29; 2 Thess. 1:9; Heb, 6:7-8; 9:27; Rev. 14:10-11). Hard-liners hold that only a few will be saved and most will be damned. Ultra–hard-liners say that God decided our fate ahead of time in "double *pre*destination," inscrutably saving some from the mass of humankind that deserved eternal punishment.

Light and No Night

A more optimistic view of things called "universalism" is held by another group. This group can find texts to support its view (e.g., 1 Tim. 2:4), though not as many as those who believe in twofold destination. This view maintains that *everyone* will be saved.

Some universalists make their case on the grounds of God's goodness. How could a loving God consign anyone to perdition? Others argue that human beings are basically good, so no one deserves eternal punishment. Still others maintain the seriousness of human sin but hold that Christ has already paid the price for it, so there is no judgment "left over" for anyone.

Light Overcoming Night

The third view is harder to articulate because it strives to include the insights of the other two. We saw how such a third position, combining the best of two other positions, emerged in the early centuries of debate about the Person of Christ. This hasn't happened yet in eschatology, but we propose the following as a developing ecumenical view.

The first scenario, Night and Light, makes an important point: God is *holy* love. God does not overlook wrong. Agape is *tough* love. Sin does separate us from God.

How we understand that toughness is terribly important.

Here as everywhere, we have a tendency to read into the Bible's teaching our own perspective. For example, we may be tempted to think that the courts and prisons we know are the model for a divine system of criminal justice. In the old days that meant "Off with their heads!" They gave it to us; now we'll give it to them. Although that notion has undergone certain refinements, we still tend to think of punishment as retribution. But that's a dubious and time-bound view.

The second scenario, Light and No Night, has a point too. God *is* loving. In fact, "love" is the noun and "holy" is the adjective. God is deep-down Agape. Retribution does not fit with unstinting love. But we can't sentimentalize that love, leaving out the judgment that sin is due. Nevertheless, on Calvary God's large heart *absorbed* the punishment all of us deserved. And this has tremendous implications for final Judgment.

Putting the two scenarios together means first of all that we can't drop the adjective "holy" from the being of God: a holy love will hold unholy sinners accountable. There *is* judgment and damnation. But the exclusive stress on holiness needs to be corrected by the divine noun, "Love." Accountability to God is not vindictive or retributive! It is *rehabilitative*. We can be *cleansed* by the burning coals of God's love, just as Isaiah's lips were cleansed in his temple encounter with the holiness of God (Isa. 6:1-7). Purification is *painful*. God's love is like a refiner's fire (Mal. 3:2-3), the burning away of dross (1 Cor. 3:13-15). Scripture does not have a "purgatory" for "venial" (little) sins dealt with by the prayers of the saints and the rites of the church. Rather, we find the simple statement of the purging love of God that "cleanses us from all sin" (1 John 1:7).

Have we made a case that *all* are saved by God's rehabilitative love? No. To blueprint universal salvation is not our business. We can't tell God what to do in the End. Nor can we deny to humans the freedom that is theirs to resist God . . . to the End. We have to do justice to both basics of the Story: God's initiative and our responsibility.

While we can't say that everyone *will be* saved, we have a right to hope that they *may be.* Universal salvation is *not* an article of faith but it can be an *article of hope.* Light is overcoming Night, but whether it will include the emptying of hell itself is God's choice . . . and ours.

Window Four: Everlasting Life

This life ends. Eternal life lasts. When God is "all in all" (1 Cor. 15:28), all the wrongs are righted, all the flaws are mended. All the resistance to the divine intention is overcome. All the alienations and separations between God and the world and within the world — nature and nature, nature and human nature, human nature and the powers of super-nature — are over and finished. Shalom is complete! The final heaven happens.

The Bible uses a rich variety of images to picture this final reconciliation of all things. It's hard to improve on the language of the Bible when trying to speak about the mysteries of the End, so we have assembled key phrases from the book of Revelation.

The Reconciliation of Humanity with God

Blessed are the pure in heart, for they will see God. (Matt. 5:8)

Seeing God is sometimes called the "beatific vision." We finally face the One from whom we have turned. We live as intended . . . in communion with God (Rev. 4:1-3).

The Revealer describes this vision with powerful images:

I saw between the throne and the four living creatures and among the elders a Lamb standing as if it had been slaughtered. (Rev. 5:6)

And the angels and the living creatures and the elders exult:

Worthy is the Lamb that was slaughtered to receive power and wealth and wisdom and might and honor and glory and blessing! (Rev. 5:12)

To see the Light is to celebrate. The joy of thanksgiving anticipated in our worship is praise that comes from the lips of those who see the *final* Light.

The Reconciliation of Human Nature with Supernature

Seeing the Light is seeing *by* the Light as well. We see in the Light of the glory of God the brothers and sisters in Christ. All the estranged shall dwell in unity in the city of God:

The nations will walk by its light, and the kings of the earth will bring their glory into it. (Rev. 21:24)

Powers as well as persons come together, finally giving obedience and praise to their Maker and Redeemer. The Revealer describes the scene in vivid images:

[An angel] showed me the holy city Jerusalem coming down out of heaven from God. It has the glory of God and a radiance like a very rare jewel, like jasper, clear as crystal. (Rev. 21:10-11)

And all the angels stood around the throne and around the elders and the four living creatures, and they fell on their faces before the throne and worshiped God. (Rev. 7:11)

The Reconciliation of Nature

The book of Revelation places "living creatures" around the throne of God. And John declares,

> I saw a new heaven and a new earth; for the first heaven and the first earth had passed away, and the sea was no more. . . . Then the angel showed me the river of the water of life, bright as crystal, flowing from the throne of God and of the Lamb through the middle of the street of the city. On either side of the river is the tree of life with its twelve kinds of fruit, producing its fruit each month; and the leaves of the tree are for the healing of the nations. (Rev. 21:1; 22:1-2)

The New Testament continues and completes the prophetic vision of Shalom in nature in which the wolf and the lamb lie down together, the child is a friend of the snake, and the desert blooms. The creation no longer groans but rejoices:

> Then I heard every creature in heaven and on earth and under the earth and in the sea, and all that is in them, singing, "To the one seated on the throne and to the Lamb be blessing and honor and glory and might forever and ever!" (Rev. 5:13)

*　　　*　　　*

All these glimpses of the world to come are brought together in a great passage that because of its inclusivity is regularly read at Christian burials:

> Then I saw a new heaven and a new earth; for the first heaven and the first earth had passed away, and the sea was no more. And I saw the holy city, the new Jerusalem, coming down out of heaven from God, prepared as a bride adorned for her husband. And I heard a loud voice from the throne saying,

"See, the home of God is among mortals. He will dwell with them as their God; they will be his peoples, and God himself will be with them; he will wipe every tear from their eyes. Death will be no more; mourning and crying and pain will be no more, for the first things have passed away." (Rev. 21:1-4)

THE NEXT TO LAST THINGS

So the Story ends. But we have yet to connect it with another "ending question" on many minds: What happens to me when I die? What about this *semi*-finale? And while we're at it, there is still an immense stretch of future to deal with, all our little tomorrows before the Great Tomorrow — 1999, the year 2000, and beyond. So eschatology is not quite over. We must speak about an *interim* future: a "postmortem" future and a historical future.

After Death

What of that midnight hour when we contemplate our approaching death? For humankind, made in the image of God, there is no way to ignore mortality. But Christians have a firm hope for our postmortem existence, sometimes called "the intermediate state." When we come to describing it, however, we have different opinions about it.

Some theologians say that we should be content with all the marvelous Last Things just described. That could mean that we right away *die into* the End . . . with the resurrection of the body, the return of Christ, the final judgment, and everlasting life. Or it could mean that there is a period of "soul sleep," a time during which we exist only in the mind of God, until a future resurrection, return, judgment, and everlasting life.

In the New Testament there are passages that speak of the "sleep" of the dead (1 Cor. 15:20; 2 Pet. 3:4, RSV). But there are also other passages that speak of the dead as very much "awake" (Luke 16:19-31; 23:43; Rev. 6:9-10). And in the Christian tradition there is a deep and long-standing sense of "the communion of saints" in the world beyond. With the emphasis on Jesus' loving pursuit—both in this world and in the world to come—of the last and the least, the writers of this book stand with the Christian tradition's belief in the union that Christ has with his people, an eternal life that begins here and now (John 5:25) and is never interrupted. The trust in this bond is expressed in Paul's memorable words:

> For I am sure that neither death, nor life, nor angels, nor principalities, nor things present, nor things to come, nor powers, nor height, nor depth, nor anything else in all creation, will be able to separate us from the love of God in Christ Jesus our Lord. (Rom. 8:38-39, RSV)

Historical Hope

The future of Christian hoping stretches far into this world as well as the next. The Next to Last Things include dreams of things to come in *this* world.

Already we have spoken a great deal about these hopes for the world of tomorrow. The doctrine of salvation anticipated them. "Sanctification" *is* the first fruit of consummation. Never perfected, always harassed by the sin it represents, it nevertheless is a hint of the final Things to Come.

But historical hope is about more than personal growth.

It's also about the big picture, hope for the world at large, for society, for nature. From the dream of Martin Luther King to the apocalyptic hopes for a thousand-year reign, Christians have believed that God has not given up on the future of this world. To pray with Christ for the Kingdom to come on earth is to believe possible a time of greater justice and peace and some respite for the battered earth. And to believe in that future is to be energized to work for it. Hope mobilizes!

How much of the Kingdom of God can we expect in this fallen world? Will we get just a whiff of the great eschatological Banquet? Or perhaps an aperitif? Or will it be the first course? Or perhaps even the main course? Christians differ. The modest but confident "soup and salad" view expresses the visionary realism we have stressed in our chapter on salvation. Yet all Christians have hope for history as well as confidence in its fulfillment at the End. And the future that God promises pulls them toward it. That is why Christian eschatology is inseparable from Christian ethics.

*   *   *

God had a Dream. And it will come true. The Power of God will assure the fulfillment of the Purpose of God.[1] The Story moves from creation to consummation. And its Author and Finisher stands revealed. The Epilogue is the Story's disclosure of Who that is.

---

1. Cf. *The Christian Story,* rev. ed. (Grand Rapids: Wm. B. Eerdmans, 1984), pp. 222-49.

QUESTIONS TO CONSIDER

1. You see a television preacher explaining the details of the imminent end of the world. How does this compare with the classical Christian view of things?

2. Some say that the best we can hope for after death is that the spiritual part of us survives while the body goes into the ground. How does this square with Christian teaching?

3. What do you think of "universalism"? Or "double predestination"? Is there another view?

4. Is our view of eternal life related to our ethics? If so, in what way?

5. What is your belief about the "intermediate state"?

6. How much hope do you have for progress toward righteousness in this world?

God

The theologian Augustine prayed, "Our hearts are restless until they find their rest in thee." We have come to a resting place. By what God has done throughout the Story, we have learned something of what Christians believe can be known about God. *Knowing* God, in Augustine's deep sense of a rested heart, is a spiritual communion that goes beyond this book's "knowing *about*" God. We pray for the deeper knowing and hope that all our theological struggles will be a step toward it.

In this Epilogue are some of the things we've learned about the chief Character in our Story. This is the doctrine of God, "theology" in its strictest sense. We speak about these things with the counsel of Scripture in mind, the reminder that we "see through a glass, darkly."

TRINITY

In the Prologue we spoke of a basic aspect of Christian belief in God: the Trinity. Now in the Epilogue it is easier to see how the church arrived at this conviction. "Threeness" takes on flesh and blood in the drama's great acts of *Creation, Reconciliation,* and *Redemption. "God the Father"* — the Maker of heaven and earth, the *Creator* — brought the world to be, providentially sustained creation in its stumble and in its fall, and entered into special covenant with it through the people of Israel. Then, at the heart of the drama, *"God the Son"* — Jesus Christ, the second Person of the Trinity, the eternal Purpose and Word — came *into* the world to reconcile it to God in the Incarnation and Atonement. *"God the Holy Spirit,"* personal Fulfiller of the Purpose, poured out the divine Power on the church, released saving graces to persons and powers in the world, and finally promises to bring all things together at the consummation. The God of Christian faith — Creator, Christ, Consummator — is one God, pursuing the vision, working out the plan, fulfilling the purpose.

At each turn in this Tale, God is fully God: The *Father* who is Creator is parenting always and everywhere, not just in Act I. *Christ* is Christ always and everywhere, not just in Act II. The *Spirit* is the Spirit always and everywhere, not just in Act III. Because God is *eternal* Father, *eternal* Son, and *eternal* Spirit, the three Persons are not just passing phases. Yet *these* Persons are unlike the kind of persons we know and are — social yet separated egos, at best relating to and at worst disconnecting from one another. God's "threeness" *is* Oneness — not a "They" or even a "We" but an "I." Life together in God is Life Together *as* God. The divine communion is divine union. God is *perfect* Love.

GOD AS LOVE

God's true character as Life Together comes out in the un-folding Story. What God did for us — from beginning to end, creation to consummation — can be no better described than by the much-used and abused word "love." God's *doing* of love, rooted in the triune *being* of love, is called *"Agape."* Agape is total Self-giving. It is steadfast, unstinting, Self-emptying. Divine Love is a fearless vulnerability to the other, a readiness to receive all things as well as to give all things (1 Cor. 13). Agape is how the Persons relate to one another — a complete sharing, a mutual *indwelling*.

This divine mutuality spills out toward the world in God's will-to-be-together with us. God creates us to be part-ners! God sticks with us even when we turn away! God pursues us stubbornly, never turned aside by any rebuff. This God, in the Bible's words, is *long*-suffering. Agape is an *in-spite-of* love, *unconditional* — loving the undeserving, the unlovable, the unlovely. (It contrasts with *eros*, which is loving only the lovable.) Agape loves *sinners*. Agape loves *enemies*.

The deepest expression of God's love for the world is the *cross*. God takes into the divine heart all our rejection and its consequences. *Compassion*, suffering for and with us, is one way the New Testament describes it. God feels what we feel, experiences what we experience. Even the estrangement from God that sinners bring on themselves and the sense of abandonment that comes in its wake — even that is known and experienced by God. We hear God's own cry in Jesus' moment of dereliction:

My God, my God, why have you forsaken me? (Mark 15:34)

143

God abandoned by God! These are the extremes to which love is willing to go. Love is the breaking of God's own heart, the long-suffering compassion of God.

GOD AS HOLY

What does it take to love this way? Toughness. Tough love is determined patience — the will to stick with us all the way. God's love will never let us go. This toughness involves rigor. God's Agape is not wimpish. Agape-Love is no marshmallow. God holds us *accountable* for our rebellion, rebuff, rejection. God says "No!" to our "no!"

The reason for this rigor is righteousness. God cannot help being who God is: *holy* love. Love does not settle for less than love *from us*. When that doesn't happen, there is separation, pain, death. To turn from the Light means being in the Night. That's the Story. When the world chose to go its own way, it paid the price: all hell broke loose. When we turned on our heel, spurning God's embrace, we stumbled and fell. There is no getting away from the consequences of our choices:

> For the wages of sin is death. (Rom. 6:23)

These tough standards of righteousness are for our own good. Without the love I'm made for, "I am nothing" (1 Cor. 13:2). God is "everything" because "God *is* love." *Life* is the Agape-Shalom that the triune God is. God wants us to be as God is. Some Christians (the Eastern Orthodox) even call this goal "divinization." God wants us to be . . . godly.

But unlike many of our experiences of toughness in this world, God's toughness is accompanied by *tenderness*. God's being is a tough tenderness. And tenderness is the *noun* while tough is the *adjective*. The accountability that righteousness demands is taken into the love that God *is*. Love takes the punishment that holiness metes out. In Luther's words, the love of God overcomes the wrath of God. As we have seen in the central chapter of the Story, God in Jesus goes all the way to the cross. In this awesome event, God's justice and God's peace embrace (see Ps. 85:10, NEB). God "has it together"; God *is* together: God is Holy Love.

In the language of theology, we have been describing the "moral attributes" of God. There are other qualities of God that are revealed in the Story. Theologians have used their own words for these qualities, borrowing from philosophy and other forms of human experience. These are sometimes called the "metaphysical attributes" of God.

Before mentioning them, we should remind ourselves that whatever words we use about God can partially describe but not completely capture the divine Reality. Our experiences of such things as love, holiness, personality, and power are marked by the fallen and finite world in which we live. So when using words for these experiences in reference to God, we must take our signals from the Story. That is why our language about God is always *analogy*, not exactitude.

GOD AS PERSONAL

How can God be Holy Love without being personal? God is the chief actor in this drama, the One who creates, reconciles, and redeems. God is *free* to be and to do. People get their idea of willing and choosing from their own experience of willing and choosing. Humans are neither robots nor puppets, although our genes and our environment play a big part in making us who we are. As noted in the chapter on creation, there is a plus to being human — the personal factor. We can't understand the Story unless we assume that God is at the *very least* as personal as we are — a choosing, deciding being.

But God is personal in ways that are inconceivable to mere mortals. No genes or environment shape the One who is pure Spirit (John 4:24). No sleep slows the divine Mind. No confusions hamper the divine Choice. God is free and personal in a sense far exceeding anything in our experience of freedom and personality. Further, in God we have to do with *three* Persons who are mysteriously *one* Person. The freedom and personal being of Each are so joined to the others that we have to do with the One who is free to be and to do. So we meet the mystery of the Trinity once again. God is personal in *God's way* of being Personal.

GOD AS ETERNAL AND INFINITE

Before the world was, God was. God brought time to be at creation. God outlasts the world. God is "everlasting" (Ps. 90:2). It's hard to speak of a "before" and "after," since these are themselves time-bound words. Again we use the language of our experience but alter it to fit the Story. We settle for saying that God is *eternal* and *ever*-lasting with no beginning or end.

As time came to be, so did space. At creation God "stretch[ed] out the heavens" and the earth (Ps. 104:2). Consequently, space is limited, "finite." But God is unlimited, "infinite." Here again words trip us up. How can there be Someone "beyond" space when the word "beyond" is itself spatial? We can say more about what the infinity of God is *not* than about what it is. This is why there is a long tradition in Christian thought that advises us to speak only in negatives about God ("apophatic theology"): God is *not* this, *not* that, *not* the other. This "negative theology" is a reminder that none of our language penetrates all the way into the divine life.

But the Story is first and foremost about what God *does* and *is*, not about what God doesn't do and isn't. So we put into our feeble words things that will become clear only at the Story's End. God is *infinite*.

GOD AS ALL-SUFFICIENT

"All our sins and griefs to bear . . ." As the song says, the God of holy love is *all*-sufficient. Everything that needs to get done does get done. God has all the power and all the knowledge and all the presence required to fulfill the divine purpose. What more could we want?

Some do want more. The "more" that is sought often has to do with the *kind* of all-sufficiency desired. All-sufficiency of this sort is the "take charge" type. It's what ancients saw in kings and generals. It's what moderns see in John Wayne. If that's the way it works in this world, some people reason, then an almighty, all-knowing, and ever-present God must be like a king, a general, or John Wayne — to the nth degree. Traditional theology sometimes took this tack when it coined the words "omnipotence," "omniscience," and "omnipresence" to refer to God.

147

Getting the Story straight at this point is terribly important. If we go with the world's ideas of all-sufficiency, then God begins to look different from the God we've learned about in the Great Narrative. God becomes a Someone who is responsible for all the misery there is in life and One who programs everything from all eternity. That's not what we've read and heard in the Story. So "all-sufficiency" in reference to God must mean something else. Let's see how that works in the three "omnis."

Omnipotence

God *is* almighty, omnipotent. God the Purposer has the *Power* to fulfill God's Purpose. Right here in the Trinity we get our clue about what potency — power — means: Nothing is going to stand in the way of God's goal. God the Holy Spirit has . . . is . . . that all-sufficient Power. But the *way* that end is gained is where the difference comes in. In the Story it is the way of "patience," "gentleness," "perseverance," "long-suffering." It pursues us as "the hound of heaven," according to the poet Francis Thompson. And it does so *implacably,* for "love never ends" (1 Cor. 13:8).

What we have, therefore, is God's relentless pursuit of a world in flight. The drama is filled with moves and countermoves. And at its turning point comes the decisive expression of power — the power of a *powerless* cross. Throughout the Story the power of God comes through as *vulnerability* — a letting go, a receiving love. God's power is the power of Self-*restraint* and Self-*giving,* not domination. God is no oriental potentate. God is "the crucified God."

Vulnerability means that God does not force creation into conformity. Love cannot be programmed. God wants the world to respond freely. That means that this ever-seeking Love risks the world's "No!" — and all the evil and chaos which comes in its wake. The price of a freely given love that is returned is the space that allows for nature, human nature, and supernature to go their own negative ways.

Yet in our Story this Power prevails! Patience and pursuit are the reason why. The *long*-suffering God outlasts our resistance, outruns our flight. That is why there is a last chapter to the Story, a *victorious* vulnerability.

By this reckoning and redefinition, God *is* almighty. Omnipotence is not knock-down, drag-out domination but rather the Power of powerlessness to pursue and prevail.

The Problem of Evil

We have just met the famous "problem of evil." The issue in "theodicy" is this: How do we hold together the omnipotence of God, the goodness of God, and the horrible fact of evil done by humans or occurring in nature? How can there be an almighty and all-loving God when there is so much misery in the world?

There are three standard answers. Each drops out one of the three "omni" assertions:

1. God *is* all-loving but not all-powerful. We have to learn to accept the fact that this "finite" God cannot bring the Kingdom and right every wrong. We have to put up as best we can with God's limitations.

2. God *is* all-powerful and can do what an all-powerful deity wants to do. That means that God does things which we may think are bad but which fit the mysterious ways of God, or which involve suffering inflicted because we sinners deserve it.

3. God is both almighty and all-loving and therefore everything really is as it should be. What we perceive to be evil or suffering either involves misapprehension on our part or is for our own benefit and thus not really evil.

The first view eliminates the power of God, the second the goodness of God, and the third the reality of evil. The trouble with these "solutions" is that *all* three beliefs are non-negotiable in the Christian Story. Can we keep God's power, God's goodness, and the reality of evil together? Here is one way. It has to do with reinterpreting the omnipotence of God as we have just done.

The almighty power of God is *not* instant-and-everywhere control of things, as the world defines it — the macho power of the potentate or patriarch. The cross tells us that God's power is a suffering love which patiently persists. So God gives the world maneuvering room to say "Yes" or "No" to the Great Invitation. Nature and supernature, as well as human beings, can go their way. Thus the terrible things that take place in these realms and among humankind. But God does not give up on any of creation. And the Story tells us that in the End the prayer of Jesus *is* answered and the Kingdom really *does* come. In God's ultimate Future every wrong is righted, every flaw mended, every brokenness healed. So God's loving Power in the face of real evil asserts itself over the time line of the Christian Story. It's no accident that in the face of death, Christians turn to Romans 8, where the power of God is stated in this *future* tense:

> I am convinced that neither death, nor life, . . . nor things present, nor things to come, . . . nor anything else in all creation, *will* be able to separate us from the love of God in Christ Jesus our Lord. (Rom. 8:38-39, italics added)

Christian theodicy cannot deny the reality of God's love or God's power or the world's evil. It "resists the powers of evil" in the confidence that the almighty and all-loving God will vindicate that struggle and prevail.

Omniscience

"God only knows!" The divine omniscience has worked its way into our very slang. Yes, God *is* all-knowing as well as almighty.

Some have taken this to mean that God knows everything ahead of time. If that is the case, God knew "from the beginning" everything you and I decide. In one long-standing theological argument, the Arminians (the followers of the theologian Jacobus Arminius) promoted this idea to protect our freedom of choice. They believed it was threatened by the "ultra-Calvinists" (the extreme followers of the theologian John Calvin), who so stressed the divine omnipotence that they claimed that God *decided* ahead of time who was to be saved and who was not. One way or the other, the "omnis" so understood and stressed the ahead-of-time control of God. In this view, God to really be *God* has to be a large-scale version of what we think it takes to be all-knowing and all-powerful.

God *is* all-knowing. God knows everything that has to be known to accomplish the divine goal. And God knows that End will be achieved — the main point of the concepts of "foreknowledge" and "foreordination." But that kind of all-knowing does *not* require God to use the divine ability to know what is in our hearts and minds ahead of time. If the Lord says, "Choose this day whom you will serve" (Josh. 24:15), that's a *real* request. We are not automatons or robots whose attitudes and behavior have been determined ahead of time. God's challenge is no charade. The Story is real *drama*. The answer could be "Yes" or it could be "No." God waits upon that response to determine the next moves of a resolute Love.

Again, we must remind ourselves of God's character of Self-restraint. God *could be* omniscient in the way our human instincts want deity to be, just as divine omnipotence *could be* our version of it. Yet, *given who God is* — utterly free, Self-giving Love — the form that God's power and knowledge take will be fitting to that nature. The free and loving God gives us the space to reply in kind. The God who could be an oriental potentate chooses otherwise. The divine Love *limits* itself to give us room to maneuver. All-knowing means that the Hound of Heaven knows enough of the hiding places to carry on the hunt.

Omnipresence

God is *everywhere*. The psalmist cries,

> Where can I flee from your presence? (Ps. 139:7)

God is everywhere we choose to go in our flight and need. God tracks us to the ends of the earth:

> If I ascend to heaven, you are there; if I make my bed in Sheol, you are there. (Ps. 139:8)

Sometimes Christian theology speaks about the divine omnipresence in terms of "immanence" and "transcendence." Immanence points to God's intimate dealings with us — the presence of God in nature and in history, in the closeness of personal communion, and in the vastness of the cosmos, and God's pursuit of us into the nether regions themselves. Yet we know that God is not reduced to this "withinness" of things and people. God is beyond space and time, whatever was, is, and will be. So God is "transcendent" as well.

But the heart of the matter is not location. The divine omnipresence, like its partners, is not a macho quality. God is *sufficiently* present for all our needs. That includes God's presence in our *flight* as well as our want. No more, no less.[1]

MYSTERY AND MEANING

We've come a long way. This telling of the Story is now over. Its adventure is unequaled. We hope you have caught some of the excitement and will share it with others. We do have a "Story to tell to the nations"!

As we sing and say it, we can never forget that we do so always by the light of our stained-glass windows. Mystery keeps company with meaning. We are still short of the End, when we shall see God "face to face." So St. Paul's wise words about modesty in our theology should always be right there along with our words and thoughts and books about the basics:

> O depth of wealth, wisdom, and knowledge in God! . . . Who knows the mind of the Lord? . . . Source, Guide, and Goal of all that is — to him be glory forever! Amen." (Rom. 11:33-34, 36, NEB)

1. Cf. *The Christian Story,* rev. ed. (Grand Rapids: Wm. B. Eerdmans, 1984), pp. 250-65.

QUESTIONS TO CONSIDER

1. Some say that more atheists are made by watching innocent people suffer than by all the scientific arguments in the world. How can there be a good and almighty God when so much evil and suffering occurs? What's your answer to this question of "theodicy" in the light of the Story and Christian teaching about God?

2. What happens to the Story when either the love of God or the holiness of God gets left out?

3. What do you think about the Trinity now that we've come to the end of the Story?

4. What is your own belief about God?

Authority and Revelation

THE BIBLE

Since the earliest centuries, Christians have returned for direction, ever and again, to a collection of stories, chronicles, sermons, genealogies, poems, hymns, and letters. Why?

The reason is that for Christians this *Bible* is the source of their Story. Here is the record of what God did, is doing, and will do to turn the world around. The events so described are understood to be the unveiling of what is ultimately real, true, and good — "revelation." Because Night has descended on our rebel world, God's special Light must pierce the gloom — with what is called *special* revelation (in contrast to *general* or *universal* revelation, which gives enough small reflections of light to all to make and keep life liveable—the Noachic covenant). So the *deeds* God does to reconcile the world are also *disclosures* of God.

There are witnesses to these deeds and disclosures — "prophets and apostles." These seers have been given special light to understand and interpret the acts of God. So the 66 books in two Testaments that make up the Christian Scripture (the books included are those agreed upon ecumenically) are valued as gifts of the Spirit — in-Spirited. Just so, Christians speak of the *inspiration* of the Bible.

While believers in this Book have sometimes been tempted to think of it as a reference volume on every subject under the sun, most today hold that it exists "to tell the Story." So they read it for the Good News of the divine doings, the *substance* of Scripture—the *Gospel*. They go to the encyclopedia for their knowledge of other things. (Today there is a big debate about Scripture among "evangelicals"— between inerrantists and the proponents of infallibility.)

At the *center* of the Story is Jesus Christ. On him the whole drama turns. Therefore, what the great Narrative means is read through the lens of Christ. Put another way, Christ, the very "Word of God," speaks through the words of the Bible.

Christians know that the Tale of God in Scripture is told in the language and thought forms of ancient times. Nevertheless, the Word gets through to us. Ordinary folk can grasp its essential meaning. But careful study of the circumstances in which the Bible was written and passed on to us is a big help too. Thus the important work of biblical scholarship. And Christians also understand that the old, old Story found in Scripture has to be related to the world in which we live today. All this means that the Bible has to be interpreted with care . . . and prayer, a practice called hermeneutics.

THE CHURCH

Sometimes it is said that "the Bible is the church's book." Certainly Scripture rose from within the people — two peoples, Israel and the early Christian community. This means that Christians need others to help us in our effort to discern the Book's meaning. Again, the Spirit comes into the picture. A gift of discernment is given by the Spirit to the Christian community — *illumination*. The light so given opens the eyes of the believer, who is given *insight* in this world and *sight* of the Truth in the world to come. Thus the church is a *resource* for understanding the *source* of the Story.

Who is this "church" that gives us this guidance? Some say it is primarily the official leadership. But even those who so limit this "teaching office" believe that true wisdom is to be traced in the end to "the whole people of God" as they have prayed, studied, and lived with Scripture. Indeed, many Christians now hold that we need the variety of viewpoints that make up the ecumenical church to hear the Word that God wants to speak to us in the pages of the Bible. Finally, God will say what God wants to — the Spirit does the illumining — but the Word comes to persons in their life together.

Of special value in hearing that Word have been the agreements reached over the centuries by the universal church, or large parts of it, on certain fundamental convictions. This lore is called "tradition." Although couched in the language of another day, it has had an abiding influence. From the ecumenical creeds of the church, for example, and other historic confessions of faith we get many of the "basics" that are in this book. As human formulations they have to be re-thought and re-stated in new times and places, but they do serve us well as *guides* to the continuing *interpretation* of the Gospel.

THE WORLD

The church lives with its Book in the *world*. It can hardly do otherwise, shaped as it is by the circumstances of its own time and place. It's important to remember how much we are influenced by that world in our reading of the Bible, for our own agenda regularly creeps into our interpretation of Scripture. That's one big reason to get the help of our sisters and brothers to correct our personal bias.

But the church *chooses* to be in the world as well. The reason again is the Spirit, the Spirit of the triune God and, therefore, the "Spirit of Christ." The church's Book tells the Christian that Christ is actively at work in the *setting* of the world. In spite of the Night that has obscured the Light, glimpses of truth are given in the rough-and-tumble of daily living. The Word is busy in the world! Wherever there is evidence of the "truth, goodness, and beauty" in Noah's covenant, there Christ through the Spirit leaves his signs. Just because it is this *hidden* Christ so present — the *impartation* of "common grace," as it's sometimes described, or Christ's "general revelation" — the *revealed* Christ of Scripture is needed to judge and interpret our perception of these *signs* in human experience. And the church also plays its part in the act of discernment.

Both our hidden biases and the viewpoint on life we have developed from our experience make up our "perspective." Getting at the basics involves moving from that setting through the resource of the church to the source (Scripture)—and back again.

When it comes to applying our understanding of authority and revelation to the Bible, here is a way to approach a verse or a passage, a way to engage in "exegesis":

1. Start with its *common*-sense meaning — reading it just like a newspaper story. But do it with others in the community of faith to get the larger view.

2. Next check out the ideas of some of the students of Scripture — the biblical scholars — who go into the back-

grounds, language, and literary style of the text. This is called the *critical* sense.

3. Now put what you've learned together with the Story and its center, Christ, especially anything in the Story that relates to the subject dealt with in the text you're reading. The basic test of what a verse or passage means is how its meaning according to common sense and critical sense fits the meaning according to this overall *canonical* sense.

4. Finally, we have to ask what Scripture means to us personally and to us in our time and place. This is the *contextual* sense that brings the Word home.

*　　　　*　　　　*

Bible, Church, World — *source, resource, setting.* These are the ways of author-izing the Story. This "where" of the matter — *authority* — is based on the "why" of the matter — *revelation.* The Bible is the source because it is inspired testimony to the revelatory deeds and disclosures of God. The Church is the resource because its interpretation and insight are gifts of the Spirit's illumination. The World is the setting because the same Spirit imparts to human experience glimpses of the divine purpose in general revelation, as rightly discerned by the lens of the biblical Christ.

We conclude this Afterword with some ways to visualize the overall structure of *authority* and the journey of *revelation.*[1]

1. Cf. *The Christian Story,* rev. ed. (Grand Rapids: Wm. B. Eerdmans, 1984), pp. 1-55; *The Christian Story,* vol. 2: *Authority: Scripture in the Church for the World* (Grand Rapids: Wm. B. Eerdmans, 1987), *passim.*

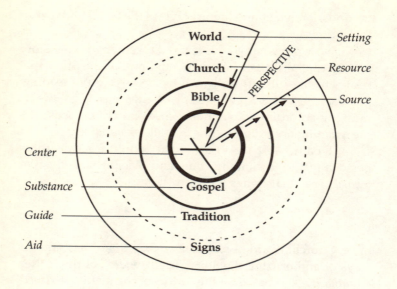

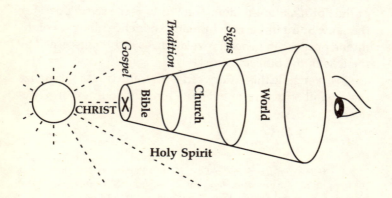

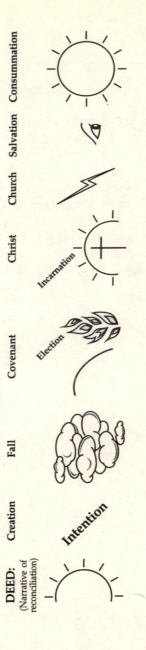

DEED:
(Narrative of
reconciliation)

Creation   Fall   Covenant   Christ   Church   Salvation   Consummation

Intention

Election

Incarnation

QUESTIONS TO CONSIDER

1. Why has the church always said that the Bible is the source of authority?

2. Does the church play a role for you in matters of authority?

3. What for you is the place of general human experience (reason, feeling, moral insight) in matters of faith?

4. Do you read the Bible through the lens of Christ? If so, what is the implication of that for some of the "difficult" passages in Scripture?

5. Do you have a way of interpreting the Bible? What is it?

Glossary / Index

Abraham xv, 29-30

    The Hebrew patriarch (married to Sarah) with whom God initiated the covenant with the Jewish people (Gen. 17:1-21).

Agape 49, 56-57, 111, 112, 131, 143-44

    God's unconditional, "in-spite-of" love for a rebellious world, and the standard of a Christian care for others that doesn't depend on merit or return.

angels 15-16, 25, 135

    Biblical powers created to be ministering agents of God (Exod. 23:20).

anthropology 10-14

    The theological doctrine of human nature.

anti-Christ 129-30

    A figure symbolizing radical opposition to Christ, often associated with the last days of the world. Theologically the existence of an anti-Christ at the End represents the Christian rejection of the theory of automatic progress (2 John 7).

apocalyptic 125, 128-29

    A word used to describe highly symbolic portions of Scripture (especially in Daniel and Revelation) and comparable movements in church history that stress the catastrophic "when," "where," "who," and "how" aspects of the end of the world.

apophatic theology 147

    A "negative theology" that accents the divine mystery by saying who and what God is not. It is distinguished from "cataphatic theology" or "positive theology," which seeks to say who and what God is.

Apostles' Creed 100, 127, 130

The present form of a second-century baptismal confession. Its three paragraphs express the three acts of the Christian drama: creation by the first Person ("the Father, the Almighty"), reconciliation in the second Person ("his only Son"), and sanctification through the third Person ("the Holy Spirit").

Arminianism 151

The teaching of Jacobus Arminius (1560-1609) that rejects the doctrine of predestination by making a place for human choice in the journey of faith.

Atonement 45-54, 62, 98

The at-one-ment of God with an alienated world — a reconciliation accomplished in the life, death, and resurrection of Christ through his prophetic, priestly, and royal ministries.

authority 155-62

The place or places to which one turns to determine Christian truth: Scripture, tradition, and human experience, usually consulted in that order of priority in classical Christian teaching.

baptism 70, 72-74, 83

A sacrament or ordinance of the church that brings (by intention, through the administration of water and the invoking of the triune Name of God) the baptized person within range of redeeming grace and into the membership and ministry of the church.

Bible viii, x, 3-4, 64, 155-62

The authoritative source of Christian basics. There is ecumenical agreement on a canon of 39 Old Testament books and 27 New Testament books.

bishop 84-85

A "pastor of pastors" usually having administrative and theological responsibilities for a designated region of the church. Some traditions hold that a succession of bishops from apostolic times assures the continuity and unity of the church (1 Tim. 3:1).

Calvary 47-49, 57, 59, 93

The place of Christ's crucifixion and the central Christian symbol of the world's reconciliation.

Calvin, John (1509-1564) 54, 151

A major figure of the Reformation remembered for his stress upon God's sovereignty and for his outline of basic Christian doctrine in the *Institutes of the Christian Religion.* Churches of the Reformed tradition trace their lineage to his teaching.

charismatic 66

In religious usage, one who believes that the supreme sign of the Holy Spirit's continuing work is "the gift of tongues" or glossolalia (mixed speech) and who practices exuberant prayer and praise.

Christ 38-63

The central figure of Christian faith, the eternal Word and Son of God, who lived among us as Jesus of Nazareth.

Christ, Person of 40-45

The classical Christian teaching of *who* Jesus is vis-à-vis God. In the Christian tradition this doctrine of the *Incarnation* describes the Person of Christ in the formula "truly God, truly human, truly one."

Christ, Work of 45-62

The classical Christian teaching of *what* Jesus Christ did to reconcile the world to God. In a widespread tradition of the church, this doctrine of *Atonement* describes the Work of Christ as the "threefold office": prophetic, priestly, and royal.

Christology 38-63

The study of the Person and Work of Christ.

confirmation 73

A rite in many churches in which a baptized person professes faith in Christ at the age of discretion, and the church blesses and the Holy Spirit confirms the baptismal action and the personal commitment. In Eastern Orthodoxy, confirmation and infant baptism take place at the same time.

consummation 125-40

The concluding chapter of the Christian Story, when the power of God brings to be the purposes of God in the *eschaton,* the End of all things.

conversion 78, 80

The Holy Spirit's transformation of a person; an "about-face" with its turning points often identified as repentance, belief, baptism, and service.

covenant xv, 27-37, 118-23

A binding agreement between or among parties. In divine-human relations, it entails God's initiative and pledge of faithfulness, and humankind's response of trust and obedience. In human relationships such as marriage or church ties, covenant is mutual faithfulness.

death 50-51, 58-59, 126-27, 137-38

A term used theologically in two senses — to refer to mortality or separation from God.

diakonia 68, 74, 76, 86-88

"Service" as a sign of the Spirit in the Body of Christ and a ministry of the church to human need — "doing the Story."

doctrine(s) x

Teachings about God and the world that are key convictions of Christian faith.

Eastern Orthodox 54

Churches of the East (Greek, Russian, etc., and ancient patriarchates such as those of Antioch and Jerusalem). Separated from the Western church in the eleventh century, they acknowledge the primacy of the patriarch of Constantinople and are known for their liturgical richness and use of icons.

ecclesiology 64-89

The doctrine of the church, its nature and mission.

ecumenical 54, 94, 157

A view of the church and its faith that seeks to overcome inherited divisions and strives for unity in witness and service (John 17:21).

eros 118, 143

A love that is given in proportion to the benefits derived. (Cf. *Agape.*)

eschatology 125-40

The Christian doctrine of the future, including both prospects

166

within history and final hopes and expectations for life after death and at the end of time.

eschaton   125

Greek for "the last thing," the consummation of God's purposes — the final chapter in the Christian Story.

eternity, eternal   51, 142, 146-47

Words used to indicate that the being and character of God are beyond the limits of time.

ethics   111-24

Right attitudes and conduct toward the other, whether persons or nature; sometimes distinguished from "morality" in that ethics is the framework for defining right moral attitudes and conduct.

eucharist / holy communion / Lord's Supper   70-72

The sacrament or ordinance in which the church gives thanks for God's saving deeds and the communicant encounters Christ's real presence in its actions, elements (bread and cup), and proclaimed Word. The observance nurtures the believer's faith and calls the church to unity and mission.

Evangel   xi-xiii, 77, 156, 160, et passim

The Good News, the Gospel, the Christian Story in its entirety, from creation to consummation; or its center in the reconciling Person and Work of Jesus Christ.

evangelical   94, 156

The name originally taken by Protestants during the Reformation who were advocates of salvation by faith alone and the supreme authority of the Bible. Today the word is used to describe those who stress a personal experience of salvation by faith alone, the rigorous use of the Bible, personal morality, and evangelistic outreach.

evangelism   78-82

Sharing the faith with those outside the church — "telling the Story" that draws persons to Christ, into the church, and toward the neighbor in need.

evil   18-26, 49-52

The state of things opposed to God and the purposes of God.

Evil, Devil   14-16, 25, 50

Created Power become perverse, personified as Satan.

exegesis 158-59

The discernment of the meaning of a verse or passage of Scripture by applying chosen principles of interpretation (e.g., "common sense," "critical sense," "canonical sense," etc.).

exemplarism 46-47

The theory of the Atonement which holds that we can be reconciled to God by following Jesus' example and teaching.

faith 93-94, 99-100

In its distinctive Christian usage, "faith" means the trust of the heart and the belief of the mind that God has forgiven our sin through the Work of Christ. More generally, "faith" means the confident trust in the will and way of God rather than the pursuit of a self-centered life.

finitude 13-14, 146-47

The condition of being limited or mortal.

fundamentalism 19

A word describing religious movements that tend to sharply separate those perceived to be true believers from those perceived to be false believers. Protestant fundamentalism (what is most often meant when the word is used) holds that the espousal of the "inerrancy" of Scripture is the basic dividing line between the faithful and the unfaithful.

Galilee 46-47, 53

The principal setting of Jesus' preaching, teaching, and healing ministry.

general (or universal) revelation 28-29, 99, 155, 157-61

The fragmentary disclosure of the purposes of God available to fallen humanity (in the evidences of nature, history, and conscience); a partial revelation accessible to all that makes life liveable, associated in Scripture with the covenant with Noah.

grace 31, 47, 93-95, 99-100, 130-31

God's special favor and power that flows from the Work of Christ toward sinners and sufferers. "Common grace" refers to God's universal favor and power that sustain creation.

heaven 15, 112-14, 121, 123, 134-38

The realm of God and final destination of the redeemed.

hell 113-14, 120-23, 131-34

The state of separation from God in the world to come.

heresy 44

A belief at odds with accepted doctrine; often a half-truth. Examples: the teaching of the Ebionites, the Adoptionists, and the Arians, who stressed Christ's humanity to the point of denying or qualifying his divine nature; and the teaching of the Docetists, the Apollinarians, and the Monophysites, who stressed Christ's divinity at the expense of his human nature.

hermeneutics 156, 158-59

The art and science of interpreting the Bible.

Holy Spirit xiv, 1-4, 66-82, 88, 93-94, 142

The Power of God as the third Person of the Trinity.

idolatry 19-20

The worship of false gods.

illumination 157, 161

The work of the Holy Spirit in the church and in believers which opens the eye of faith to truth, here and hereafter.

image of God xi, 10-12

Variously described in theology as the special relation, capacity, or call given by God to all humans; "imaging God" is the faithful response to this gift.

immanence (of God) 152-53

God's presence and activity in creation.

impartation 158, 161

A term used in this book for God's universal disclosure of enough light and truth to make life liveable for all and to allow the Story to go forward — "general revelation."

Incarnation 40-45, 49, 51-52, 62, 98-99

The coming of God's Word, the second Person of the Trinity, in the flesh as Jesus Christ; sometimes called "the doctrine of the Incarnation."

inerrancy 19, 67-68, 156

An interpretation of the Bible that holds it to be without error in everything about which it speaks, including matters of science and history. There are divisions within this school of thought determined by the degree to which the role of human authorship is acknowledged.

infallibility 156

An interpretation of the Bible which holds that it is trustworthy in matters of theology and morality but subject to error in matters of science and history. There are divisions within this school of thought and often sharp controversy with exponents of inerrancy.

infinity, infinite 146-47

Words used to indicate that the being and character of God are not limited by space.

inspiration 156, 159, 161

The work of the Holy Spirit that enables biblical seers — "prophets and apostles" — to report and interpret the deeds of God in a trustworthy way.

Israel xi, 29-36, 39, 54, 67

The people with whom God establishes and continues a special covenant (Abraham, Moses, David) in order to carry out the reconciliation of creation.

Jericho Road 56

The setting of the Good Samaritan story, which symbolizes Christ's call to serve the neighbor in need (Luke 10:30-37).

justice 97, 115-17, 130ff.

In our fallen world, God's purpose of giving each his or her due.

justification by faith 93-95, 97, 99-100, 123-24

The teaching emphasized by the Reformation, but also held throughout Christian history, that persons are saved by grace received by trust in Christ's saving Work rather than by reliance on their good works.

kerygma 67, 74, 77, 82, 84, 88

"Proclamation" (the Greek meaning) as a sign of the Spirit and mark of the church — "telling the Story."

koinonia 69, 74, 77-78, 86, 88

"Fellowship" (the Greek meaning) or "life together" as a sign of the Spirit and mark of the church — "being the Story."

laity 85-89

Used variously to refer to the whole people of God *(laos)* or to the people of God who make up the 99 percent of the church called to a ministry distinguishable from that of the clergy.

legalism 114

The belief that moral conduct consists only of absolute obedience to the letter of the law.

leitourgia   70-72, 75, 78, 82, 84, 88

"Worship" or "liturgy" as a sign of the Spirit and mark of the church — "celebrating the Story."

liberation   31, 50, 60, 76, 81-82, 97

Deliverance from the foes that resist God's purposes. In "liberation theology" the accent is on deliverance from institutional powers of oppression (political, economic, and social) and the suffering they inflict on their victims. More generally, liberation includes freedom from the allied foes of sin, death, and error as well as from oppression.

Luther, Martin (1483-1546)   23, 65, 92-94

The figure to whom the mainstream Reformation is often traced. He is remembered for his stress upon salvation by grace alone, through faith alone. Lutheran churches trace their lineage to his teaching and influence.

Mary   43

The mother of Jesus, esteemed throughout Christian history as the human bearer of the eternal Word and the first Christian believer.

metanoia   78, 80

An "about-face" (the Greek meaning), repentance, or conversion.

millennialism   130

Belief in the thousand-year reign of Christ on earth (Rev. 20:1-10).

— **amillennialism**   The interpretation of the thousand years as symbolic of Christ's present heavenly rule in the midst of history's continuing struggle.

— **postmillennialism**   The interpretation of the thousand years as a time of peace, plenty, and evangelistic success within history before the return of Christ.

— **premillennialism**   129

The interpretation of the thousand years as inaugurated by the return of Christ and preceded by a time of tribulation.

ministry   33, 54-55, 73, 83-88

The service of God carried out by Christ and continued by the whole Body of Christ in various forms, especially as the partner ministries of laity and clergy.

miracle 55, 61-62, 76

An extraordinary event held to be a special act of God.

mission 75-82

The reach of the Body of Christ to those beyond it — the church's "outreach" in doing, telling, being, and celebrating the Story.

morality 111-24

Right attitudes and conduct toward the other, whether persons or nature. (Cf. **ethics**.)

Moses 30-31

The leader commissioned to bring Israel out of Egyptian bondage to the Promised Land and entrusted with God's covenant law.

nature 6-10, 24-25, 136-37

Creation at the level of stones and stars, atoms and animals.

Noah xv, 27-29, 99, 158, 161

The biblical figure representing God's covenant with all creation. The *Noachic covenant* is God's promise to sustain creation despite its rebellion, giving it enough light and power for the Story to go forward (Gen. 9:8-10, 12-13).

orders of creation / preservation 15, 29, 117-20

Structures of life together such as the family, the state, and the processes needed for securing food, clothing, and shelter, purposed by God for making and keeping human life liveable.

ordination 83-88

A rite in which a baptized Christian is publicly consecrated to a special calling within the ministry of the church.

original sin 20-21

The universal human tendency to turn away from God that has prevailed since the first moment of humanity's option to choose right or wrong.

paradox 45

An assertion of two mutually exclusive propositions necessitated by the theological facts or by the experience of faith.

Paul 93-94

The apostle to the Gentiles and author of various New Testament letters that lay the groundwork for certain Christian teachings such as justification by faith.

penal substitution 48

A theory of the Atonement traceable to the sixteenth century which holds that Jesus Christ paid the penalty for our sin by his death on the cross. The picture popularly presented is that the judgment of the Father was satisfied by the loving sacrifice of Jesus.

perfectionism 113-14

The belief that perfect love as going-the-second-mile, cheek-turning self-abnegation (Matt. 5:38-42) is the literal rule of conduct in human relationships.

Person 2-3, 40-45, 142, 145-46

A theological term used to describe the Father, the Son, and the Holy Spirit as subjects distinguishable within the being and doing of God yet so intimately united as to be Three in One.

pluralism 97-100

In religious usage, the variety of worldviews found in a society or epoch.

prayer 101-11

Communication with God in the varied ways of adoration, confession, thanksgiving, intercession, petition, and commitment.

predestination 132, 151

The teaching associated with traditional Calvinism which holds that the eternal destiny of all persons — their salvation or damnation — is foreordained by God. Sometimes it is described as God's rescue of some from the damnation deserved by all and God's passing over of the rest.

principalities and powers 15-16, 25, 60, 76, 81, 135

Superhuman entities created to serve God yet subject to the Fall.

prophet xi, 31-33, 54-57

One who speaks and acts for God and points with both hope and judgment to the future.

Providence 28-29

God's steadfast mercy that sustains the divine purposes in the created order and in personal lives.

real presence 71-72

The risen Christ's special meeting with the communicant in the action and elements of the holy communion/eucharist.

reconciliation   45, 54ff., 134-37, 142

The coming together of the world and God accomplished by the Work of Christ.

resurrection   50-51, 61-62, 126-27

The new state of a human being inaugurated by the raising of Jesus Christ from the dead, and the "spiritual body" for which persons are destined at the consummation.

revelation   28, 31-32, 38ff., 99, 134-35, 155-61

God's disclosure of the truth about the divine purposes described in this book as the Holy Spirit's gift of light imparted fragmentarily in a fallen creation, manifested in the election of Israel, and enacted in the Incarnation of Christ, made accessible to us through the inspiration of Scripture and its illumination in the church and the heart of the believer, here and hereafter.

sacrament   70-74

A rite of the church in which a promise of grace is symbolized by an object and an action — "an outward and visible sign of an inward and spiritual grace." Baptism and holy communion/ eucharist are two sacraments on which there is ecumenical agreement. In some traditions sacraments are called "ordinances."

salvation   xvi, 36, 45ff., 90-124

Deliverance by Christ from the foes that alienate the world and/or the individual from God (sin, evil, death, and error). The health, wholeness, and reconciliation that result in the life of the individual by grace through faith and/or in the world by grace through love.

sanctification   94-95, 124, 138

The pilgrimage of the believer in "becoming holy" after being "declared holy" in justification by faith; the power of the Spirit *in* the believer that accompanies Christ's pardon *of* the believer.

Savior   47-48, 57-59

A New Testament title for Christ that stresses his deliverance of the world from powers inimical to God's purposes — most often the power of sin. Personal confession of Christian faith is often associated with the profession of Christ as Savior (and Lord).

Shalom x, xii, 32-34, 36, 54-55, 112-13, 116, 123

A Hebrew word often translated as "peace," meaning freedom from the evil that prevents life together.

sin 18-22, 57-59, 92-95

Turning to the self as the center of the universe and away from God and the divine purposes.

situation ethics, situationalism 122-23

The belief that moral decisions are based on love's assessment of the best consequences discernible in a given situation rather than on adherence to a moral law or code.

soteriology 90-124

The Christian doctrine of salvation, either including the Work of Christ ("objective soteriology") or focusing on its application to the individual ("subjective soteriology") and its implementation in society.

soul 12-13, 126-27

The self's unique relation to God.

supernature 14-16, 25, 135

The realm beyond nature and human beings created by God, including realities (e.g.,"angels," "powers") to which Scripture testifies.

supersessionism 34-35

The belief that Israel's covenant with God has been abrogated by Christ's coming. "Anti-supersessionism" is the assertion that God's covenant with the Jewish people has not been abrogated by Christ's coming. There are many varieties of both notions.

theodicy 149-51

The problem of evil, or how to reconcile three Christian concepts that are non-negotiable: God as all-loving, God as almighty, and evil as absolutely real. In technical terms, theodicy is "the justification of God."

theology x

In general, thoughts and words about God; in Christian usage, thoughts and words in the Christian community about the teachings of the Christian faith in a given time and place.

tradition 157-58, 160

Expressions of Christian belief and practice in documents and

teachings that have been preserved over the centuries as resources for interpreting biblical faith.

transcendence (of God) 152-53

God's being and activity beyond the created order.

Trinity xiv, 2-3, 49, 141-42

The unique Christian doctrine of God — the one God as a totally
united life together of Father, Son, and Holy Spirit. The three
Persons in their eternal being have been called the "ontologi-
cal Trinity." Their special missions in the Christian drama —
creation (Father), reconciliation (Son), and sanctification (Holy
Spirit) — have been called the "economic Trinity" (the "econ-
omy" being the outworking of the divine plan).

universalism 132

The belief that every human being will finally be saved.